Eyewitness

ANCIENT GREECE

Bronze mirror cover showing Aphrodite playing knucklebones with Pan. 350 B.C.

Round mouthed jug with coins

Griffin's head *rhyton*

Bronze banqueter figurine

Aphrodite removing her sandal

Theseus and the minotaur

Kylix

Eyewitness
ANCIENT GREECE

Bronze
chariot

Written by
ANNE PEARSON

Dorling Kindersley

Wine strainer

Oil container

Bronze cymbals

Terracotta dancing woman

Terracotta figurine of a youth with hat

Griffin earrings

Rattle shaped like a pig

DK

LONDON, NEW YORK, MUNICH,
MELBOURNE, and DELHI

Project editor Gillian Denton
Art editor Liz Sephton
Senior editor Helen Parker
Senior art editor Julia Harris
Production Louise Barratt
Picture research Diana Morris
Special photography Nick Nicolls
Additional photography Liz MacCaulay

PAPERBACK EDITION
Managing editor Andrew Macintyre
Managing art editor Jane Thomas
Editor and reference compiler Lorrie Mack
Art editor Catherine Goldsmith
Production Jenny Jacoby
Picture research Jo Haddon
DTP designer Siu Ho

This Eyewitness ® Guide has been conceived by
Dorling Kindersley Limited and Editions Gallimard

Hardback edition first published in Great Britain in 1992.
This edition published in Great Britain in 2002
by Dorling Kindersley Limited,
80 Strand, London WC2R ORL

A CIP catalogue record for this book is
available from the British Library.

ISBN 0 7513 4738 8

Colour reproduction by
Colourscan, Singapore
Printed in Hong Kong by Toppan

See our complete
catalogue at
www.dk.com

Contents

Child's toy

The Greek world

THE LAND OF GREECE is made up of mainland Greece and the numerous islands scattered throughout the Aegean and Adriatic Seas. It is a mountainous country with hot dry summers and rain only in winter. The early Greek settlements developed as small independent communities cut off from each other by the mountains and often competing for the best land, because the fertile arable soil is in short supply. Each of the city-states which developed out of these communities had a strong individual identity, and citizens were very loyal to their home state and to its patron deity. This miscellaneous collection of city-states sometimes joined together for mutual defence and did so most successfully against the Persians. The Greeks produced a glorious culture which has had a profound effect on western civilization through succeeding centuries, reverberating right down to the present day. They scaled the heights in literature, the visual and dramatic arts, in philosophy and politics, in sport, and in many other aspects of human life. Greek civilization reached its peak in Athens in the fifth century B.C.

KOUROS
Kouroi (marble statues of naked boys), were made mainly in the sixth century B.C. to decorate sanctuaries of the gods, especially Apollo, but some may have been put up in memory of young soldiers who had died in battle. They stand with their arms by their sides and one foot in front of the other.

THE ANCIENT
GREEK WORLD
This map shows ancient Greece and the surrounding area. It includes towns established by the first emigrants from the mainland who travelled east. The emigrants settled on the coastal area of Asia Minor called Ionia. The names of the regions are in capitals and the cities are in small letters.

THRACE

MACEDON

Troy

Pergamum

AEGEAN SEA

LYDIA

Delphi

Plataea   Thebes   Smyrna

Eleusis   IONIA

Corinth   Athens

Ephesus

IONIAN   Tiryns   Miletus

SEA   Olympia   Mycenae   CARIA

N   Didyma

Halicarnassos   Theangela

Sparta   LYCIA

Phylakopi

Akrotiri   Camirus

CRETE   Knossos   Mallia   SCALE

Zakro   Km   150

Phaistos   Miles   100

6

ACROPOLIS
The city of Athens (pp. 16–17) was the most important city of ancient Greece, and the main centre for all forms of arts and learning. Its Acropolis was crowned with the temple of the Parthenon, dedicated to the goddess Athena.

DONKEY DRINKING CUP
Beautifully painted pottery was a speciality of the Greeks. It was used mainly for storing, mixing, serving, and drinking wine. This is a special two-handled cup in the form of a donkey's head.

HIPPOCAMP
This gold ring is decorated with a hippocamp, a sea horse with two forefeet and a body ending in the tail of a dolphin or a fish.

GREECE AND THE WIDER WORLD
This chart shows the rise and fall of the Greek world from Minoan times to the end of the Hellenistic period. These historic events can be seen against a background of other civilizations in Europe, Asia, and South America.

DATES B.C.	2000–1500	1500–1100	1100–800	800–480	480–323	323–30
EVENTS IN GREECE	Cretan palace civilization	Fall of Knossos. Rise and fall of Mycenaean civilization.	The foundation of Sparta The formation of Homeric poems	Ionian and Black Sea colonies founded First Olympic Games	Persian invasions Start of democracy in Athens Sparta controls the Peloponnese Age of Perikles	Rise of Macedon Fall of Sparta Life of Alexander Wars of Alexander's successors
CULTURAL PERIOD	Bronze age	Bronze age	Dark age	Archaic	Classical	Hellenistic
WORLD EVENTS	Indus Valley civilizations in India Middle Kingdom in Egypt	Egyptian New Kingdom Babylonian empire Mayan civilization in central America Chang dynasty in China	Celtic peoples arrive in Britain Phoenician colonies in Spain Olmec civilization in Mexico	Rise of Etruscans in Italy Kushites invade Egypt Rome founded Assyrian empire	Confucius born in China Assyrians conquer lower Egypt Persian empire	Toltecs settle in central Mexico Ch'in dynasty in China Great Wall built in China

MARATHON MEN
Athletics was a favourite pastime in ancient Greece (pp. 44–45). Games took place as part of religious festivals. These three runners are painted on a pot which was given as a prize to the winner of the race at the Panathenaic Games held in Athens in honour of Athena (pp. 16–17).

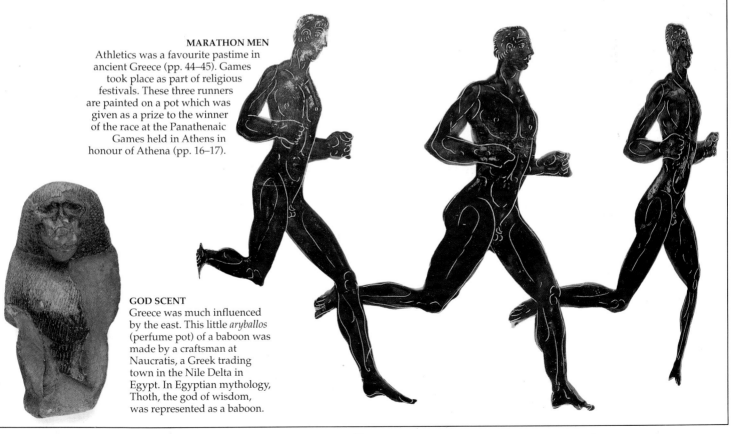

GOD SCENT
Greece was much influenced by the east. This little *aryballos* (perfume pot) of a baboon was made by a craftsman at Naucratis, a Greek trading town in the Nile Delta in Egypt. In Egyptian mythology, Thoth, the god of wisdom, was represented as a baboon.

Minoan civilization

THE FIRST GREAT CIVILIZATION of the Aegean world flourished on the island of Crete. The early inhabitants settled as early as 6000 B.C., but the island reached the height of its power between 2200 B.C. and 1450 B.C. Its wealth was due to its thriving trade with other Bronze Age towns in Greece, the Mediterranean, and in Egypt and Syria. Prosperity also came from the rich Cretan soil which produced oil, grain, and wine in abundance. The economy was based around rich palaces, the remains of which have been found in different parts of the island. This peaceful Cretan civilization is known as Minoan after a legendary king of Crete called Minos. Knossos and the other palaces were all destroyed by fire in about 1700 B.C., but after that they were rebuilt even more luxuriously. From then until about 1500 B.C., Minoan civilization was at its height.

DECORATING WITH DOLPHINS
The walls of the Minoan palaces were richly decorated with painted scenes known as frescoes, made by applying paint to wet plaster. Many we see today are modern reconstructions based on fragments of painted plaster which have survived. This famous dolphin fresco is from the Queen's apartment at Knossos.

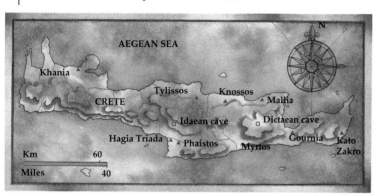

CRETE
This map shows the main towns and palaces on the island, at Knossos, Zakro, Phaestus, and Mallia. A large villa has also been found at Hagia Triada. Most of the settlements were built close to the sea. The remains of the lavish buildings are evidence of the skill of Minoan architects, engineers, and artists. Not everyone lived in the palaces. Some lived in smaller town houses or in farmhouses in the country. It is said that the young Zeus was brought up in the Dictaean Cave on the high plain of Lassithi.

WORSHIPPER
This bronze figure is in an attitude of worship of the gods.

TAKING THE BULL BY THE HORNS
The bull was regarded by the Minoans as a sacred animal. A Greek myth tells the story of the god Zeus falling in love with a beautiful princess called Europa. Zeus turned himself into a white bull and swam to Crete with her on his back. They had three sons, one of whom was Minos who became the king of Crete. Daring bull sports became a way of worshipping the bull. This bronze figure shows a boy somersaulting over the bull's horns.

BULL MURAL
This mural at Knossos also shows an acrobat leaping the bull.

DISCOVERING KNOSSOS
English archaeologist Sir Arthur Evans (1851–1941) discovered the biggest and most famous of the Minoan palaces at Knossos in 1894. He dug there for several years and the remains of the colossal building with its hundreds of rooms amazed the world.

THESEUS AND THE MINOTAUR
According to Greek legend a young prince of Athens called Theseus went to Crete and killed a monster, half-man and half-bull, to whom Athenian children were sent as sacrifice each year. The monster, the Minotaur, was kept in a maze called the Labyrinth. It is possible that the huge palace at Knossos may have resembled a Labyrinth because of its many long and winding corridors.

MODERN MINOTAUR
The story of the conflict between Theseus and the Minotaur was popular not only with Greek vase painters but also with many modern artists. This interpretation by Spanish artist Pablo Picasso (1881–1973) is almost as difficult to unravel as the maze!

RESTORATION AND RECONSTRUCTION
The palace of Knossos was built and rebuilt several times. It was made of stone with wooden roofs and ceilings. Some parts of it were four storeys high. It had royal apartments including a throne room where the ruler of Knossos would sit in splendour. Sir Arthur Evans restored some of the palace so that it is possible to get a sense of what it was like when it was new. The wooden columns are painted the same shade of red as the original.

The Mycenaean civilization

GREECE IN THE BRONZE AGE (before iron tools and weapons came into use), had several important centres, including Mycenae. Mycenae, city of Agamemnon, was one of several heavily fortified strongholds. The king, or chief, lived in a palace with many rooms which served as a military headquarters and a centre of administration for the surrounding countryside. The Mycenaeans were warriors, and weapons and armour have been found in their graves. They were also great traders and sailed far and wide. Their civilization reached the height of its power in about 1600 B.C. and eclipsed the Minoan civilization of Crete. All seemed secure and prosperous, but around 1250 B.C. the Mycenaeans started to build huge defensive walls around all the major towns. The Mycenaean world was under threat from foreign invaders. By about 1200 B.C. the cities began to be abandoned or destroyed. Within 100 years the Mycenaean strongholds had fallen and a period often called the Dark Ages had begun.

POMEGRANATE PENDANT
This little gold pendant in the form of a pomegranate was found in Cyprus. It was made by a Mycenaean craftsman around 1300 B.C. and is a good example of a jewellery technique called granulation. Tiny gold granules grouped in triangles decorate the surface of the pomegranate. Mycenaean artists and traders settled in Cyprus in large numbers. The island later provided a refuge for many Greeks fleeing from unrest at home, as Mycenaean civilization crumbled.

BULL SPRINKLER
This clay bull's head was used as a ritual sprinkler at religious ceremonies. There are small holes in the mouth to let the water escape. Although these sprinklers are sometimes in the shape of other animals, bulls are the most common.

OCTOPUS JAR
This pottery jar with a painting of an octopus was found in a cemetery at a Mycenaean colony on the island of Rhodes. Mycenaean artists were much influenced by Minoan work and subjects like this, inspired by the sea, continued to be popular.

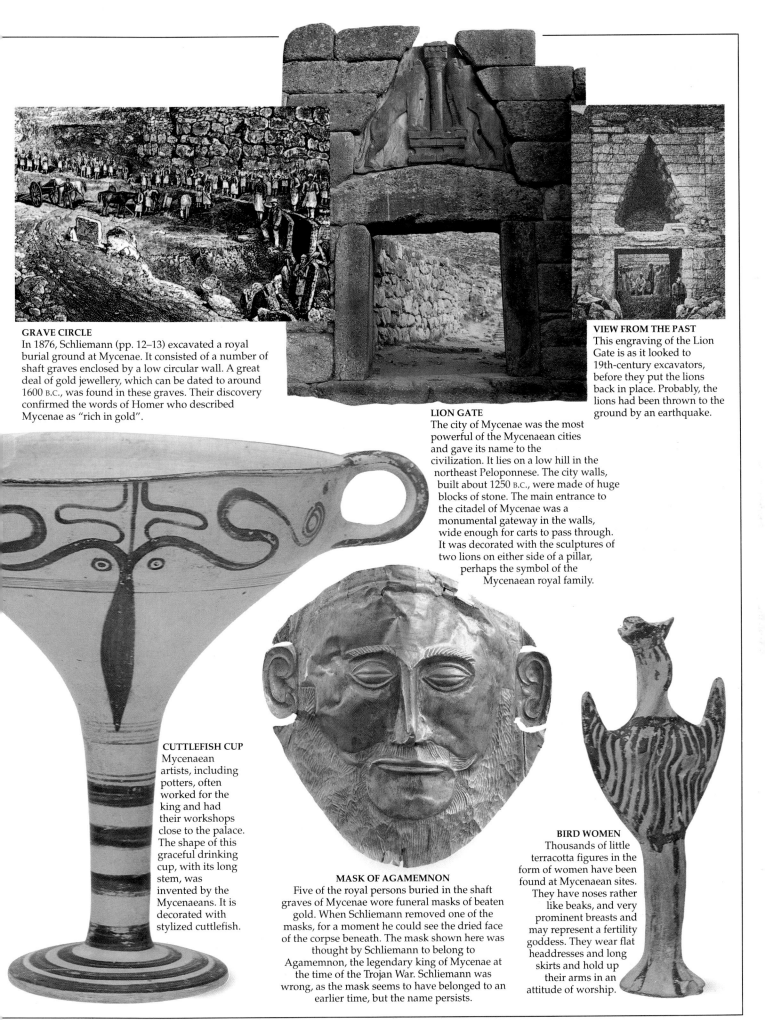

GRAVE CIRCLE
In 1876, Schliemann (pp. 12–13) excavated a royal burial ground at Mycenae. It consisted of a number of shaft graves enclosed by a low circular wall. A great deal of gold jewellery, which can be dated to around 1600 B.C., was found in these graves. Their discovery confirmed the words of Homer who described Mycenae as "rich in gold".

VIEW FROM THE PAST
This engraving of the Lion Gate is as it looked to 19th-century excavators, before they put the lions back in place. Probably, the lions had been thrown to the ground by an earthquake.

LION GATE
The city of Mycenae was the most powerful of the Mycenaean cities and gave its name to the civilization. It lies on a low hill in the northeast Peloponnese. The city walls, built about 1250 B.C., were made of huge blocks of stone. The main entrance to the citadel of Mycenae was a monumental gateway in the walls, wide enough for carts to pass through. It was decorated with the sculptures of two lions on either side of a pillar, perhaps the symbol of the Mycenaean royal family.

CUTTLEFISH CUP
Mycenaean artists, including potters, often worked for the king and had their workshops close to the palace. The shape of this graceful drinking cup, with its long stem, was invented by the Mycenaeans. It is decorated with stylized cuttlefish.

MASK OF AGAMEMNON
Five of the royal persons buried in the shaft graves of Mycenae wore funeral masks of beaten gold. When Schliemann removed one of the masks, for a moment he could see the dried face of the corpse beneath. The mask shown here was thought by Schliemann to belong to Agamemnon, the legendary king of Mycenae at the time of the Trojan War. Schliemann was wrong, as the mask seems to have belonged to an earlier time, but the name persists.

BIRD WOMEN
Thousands of little terracotta figures in the form of women have been found at Mycenaean sites. They have noses rather like beaks, and very prominent breasts and may represent a fertility goddess. They wear flat headdresses and long skirts and hold up their arms in an attitude of worship.

To Troy and back

IN THE 12TH CENTURY B.C., the rich Mycenaean towns and palaces fell into a decline or were destroyed, trade with the east decreased, and Greece entered a dark age. During the next few centuries, stories of the great Mycenaean civilization which had gone before were handed down from one generation to the next in the form of poems. Two of them, *The Iliad* and *The Odyssey*, have survived. They reached their final form in the eighth century B.C. at the hands of the poet Homer, whose poetry was admired throughout the Greek world. *The Iliad* describes how a city called Troy, on the west coast of modern Turkey, was besieged by a Greek army led by King Agamemnon of Mycenae. It describes the heroic deeds of Greek and Trojan soldiers like Achilles and Hektor. *The Odyssey* tells the story of the return home from the Trojan War of one Greek hero, Odysseus. It took him ten years and he had many dangerous adventures. The Homeric stories reflect real incidents of wars, battles, and sieges from an earlier age. It is probable that war was waged between the Greeks and the Trojans, possibly over the ownership of lands and crops at a time when the Mycenaean world was falling apart, and not over the recapture of Helen (above).

HEINRICH SCHLIEMANN
In 1870, German archaeologist Heinrich Schliemann (1822–1890), discovered the site of ancient Troy near the Mediterranean coast in modern Turkey. He had been looking for it for many years. His excavations revealed not just one city, but more than nine of them, built on top of each other. (It is not certain which layer is the city described in *The Iliad*). Schliemann's wife is wearing some of the superb jewellery found at Troy.

HELEN OF TROY
Helen was the beautiful wife of Menelaus, king of Sparta and brother of Agamemnon, king of Mycenae. According to legend, Helen's capture by Paris, son of Priam, king of Troy, was the cause of the Trojan War. The Greeks united to defeat the Trojans and restore Helen to her husband.

OVERCOME BY CURIOSITY
Troy withstood the Greeks' siege for ten long years. In the end, the Greeks triumphed by a trick. They constructed a huge wooden horse which they left just outside the city. The Trojans then watched the Greek army sail away, and overcome with curiosity, dragged the horse inside the city walls. Late that night, Greek soldiers, hidden inside the horse, crept out and opened the city gates. The Greek army, which had silently returned, entered and destroyed the city. This picture of the horse comes from a pot of about 650–600 B.C.

MODERN MODEL
In Troy today, there is a modern model of the Trojan horse. It is very large and, like the ancient one, is made of wood. Children can climb a ladder into its stomach and pretend to be Greek soldiers.

THE WOODEN HORSE
The story of Troy and the wooden horse has been a favourite with artists through the centuries. Italian artist Giovanni Tiepolo (1696–1770), painted more than one version of the subject.

THE BLINDING OF POLYPHEMUS

In one of his adventures on his way home from the Trojan war, the hero Odysseus met a Cyclops called Polyphemus, a man-eating giant with only one eye in the middle of his forehead. Odysseus and his men were trapped in Polyphemus' cave and the giant started to eat them one by one. Cunning Odysseus brought the giant a skin full of wine which lulled him into a drunken sleep. Then he blinded Polyphemus by driving a red-hot stake into his only eye.

PATIENT PENELOPE

After his ten-year journey, Odysseus returned at last to Ithaca, his island home, and to his wife Penelope. During his long absence, she had waited patiently for him, even though everyone else had given him up for dead. When other men proposed marriage to Penelope, she told them that she would give them an answer when she had finished weaving a particular piece of cloth. At night, Penelope crept secretly to her loom, and undid everything she had woven during the day. In this way, she postponed indefinitely her reply to her suitors. In this painting by British artist John Stanhope (1829–1908), Penelope is sitting sadly beside her loom.

WOOLLY ESCAPE

Polyphemus kept a flock of sheep in the cave at night and these provided a means of escape. Odysseus and his men tied themselves underneath the sheep. In the morning, the flock filed out of the cave to graze. The blind giant felt the backs of the sheep in case his captives were hiding there, but he did not think of feeling under their bellies. This story has been illustrated on a black-figured vase.

Blue paint indicating sea

Helmet

MOTHER TO THE RESCUE

The mother of Achilles was a sea nymph called Thetis. This little terracotta figurine shows Thetis, or one of her sisters, riding the waves on a sea horse, bringing a new helmet for Achilles to wear in battle. Some of the bright blue paint representing the sea, still survives.

DEATH OF A HERO

After the Greek champion, Achilles, had killed the bravest Trojan warrior, Hektor, he tied his body to a chariot and dragged it three times around the walls of Troy. On this clay lamp, Achilles can be seen driving the chariot and looking back in triumph. Above him, on the walls of Troy, Hektor's parents, King Priam and Queen Hecuba, watch in horror.

Greek expansion

GREECE STARTED TO EMERGE from the Dark Ages in the eighth century B.C. Trading posts began to be established abroad, even as far away as the Nile Delta. As the population expanded and Greek agriculture proved insufficient to meet the needs of the people, some towns sent out colonies both east- and westwards. They settled in southern Italy, Sicily, and other parts of the western Mediterranean, and in the east, around the shores of the Black Sea. Some of these colonies were very rich. It was said that the people of Sybaris in southern Italy slept on beds of rose petals, and roosters were banned from the town so that the inhabitants would not be woken too early in the morning. Greek culture was influenced by foreign styles. The Geometric style, a style, as its name suggests, dominated by geometric patterns, gave way to a new, so-called Orientalizing style. Designs influenced by the East such as griffins and sphinxes, were introduced. Egypt and Syria were the main sources. Corinth, Rhodes, and Ephesus were well placed for eastern trade and became rich.

GOLDEN GRIFFINS
These gold griffin heads, inspired by the east, were found on the island of Rhodes. They were made in the seventh century B.C. and were once attached to a pair of earrings.

MAN SIZE
The Greeks liked to wear bangles decorated with animal heads. This lion-headed bangle, which is silver-plated, may have been worn by a man.

FOND FAREWELL
This detail is from a large pot decorated in the Geometric style. The figures are rather rigid and painted in silhouette. The man on the right is stepping onto a boat and taking leave of the woman. Perhaps he is meant to be the hero Odysseus saying goodbye to his wife Penelope before he goes off to the Trojan War (pp. 12–13), or possibly he is Paris abducting Helen.

FAIENCE FROG
At this time in Greek history, there was much interest in Egpytian art and the craftsman who made this may have been copying Egyptian work. It shows a man kneeling and holding a jar on top of which is a frog, a sacred creature in Egyptian religion. The object is made of faience, a greenish material often used to make Egyptian ornaments.

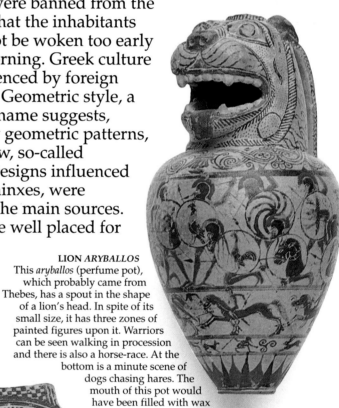

LION *ARYBALLOS*
This *aryballos* (perfume pot), which probably came from Thebes, has a spout in the shape of a lion's head. In spite of its small size, it has three zones of painted figures upon it. Warriors can be seen walking in procession and there is also a horse-race. At the bottom is a minute scene of dogs chasing hares. The mouth of this pot would have been filled with wax to prevent the evaporation of the perfume inside.

EXOTIC EXPORTS
Many little perfume pots were made in the town of Corinth and exported all over the Greek world. They are often in curious shapes and prettily decorated. This one has a winged figure painted on it who may represent a god of the wind.

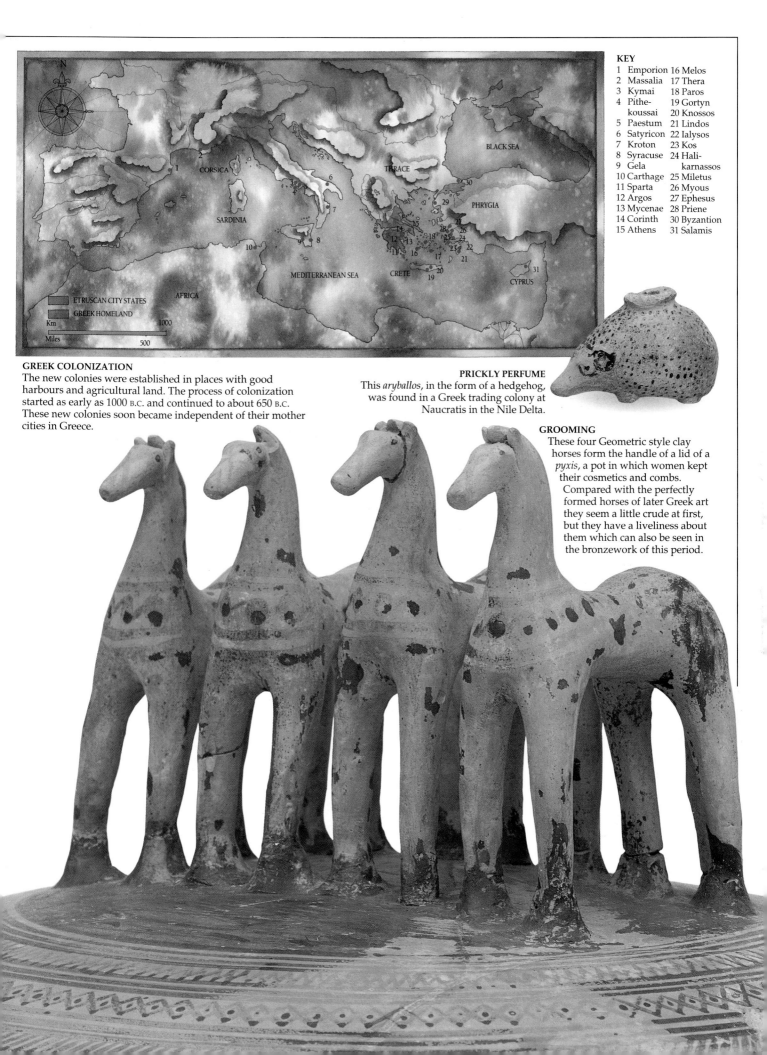

GREEK COLONIZATION

The new colonies were established in places with good harbours and agricultural land. The process of colonization started as early as 1000 B.C. and continued to about 650 B.C. These new colonies soon became independent of their mother cities in Greece.

PRICKLY PERFUME

This *aryballos*, in the form of a hedgehog, was found in a Greek trading colony at Naucratis in the Nile Delta.

GROOMING

These four Geometric style clay horses form the handle of a lid of a *pyxis*, a pot in which women kept their cosmetics and combs. Compared with the perfectly formed horses of later Greek art they seem a little crude at first, but they have a liveliness about them which can also be seen in the bronzework of this period.

Athens, city of Athena

THE ACROPOLIS
In early times, the Acropolis (high city) of Athens was a fortified citadel. Later, it became the most sacred part of the town where many important temples and sanctuaries were situated.

SACRED STATUE
The purpose of the procession shown on the frieze was to bring a new dress for a sacred wooden statue of Athena, which stood on the Acropolis. The dress, a woven *peplos* (pp. 42–43), is being handed to a priest.

ATHENS WAS THE MOST POWERFUL of all the Greek city-states. It was also a great centre of the arts and learning. Its patron Athena was goddess of wisdom and warfare and perfectly symbolized the two sides of her city's life. In 480 B.C., Athens was attacked by the Persians and the temples on the Acropolis were destroyed. Later, when Athens had played a leading role in the Persian wars (pp. 54–55) and successfully defended Greece, a huge rebuilding programme was launched by the leader of Athens, Perikles (pp. 18–19). Athens was situated in an area called Attica and was more densely populated than other Greek cities. The people of Athens lived on the land below the Acropolis. Many fine public squares and colonnaded buildings have been found there around the *agora*, an open space for meeting and commercial activity. Nearby was the port of Athens, the Piraeus. Access to the sea was a main reason for Athens' miltary and economic successes.

THE ERECHTHEION
A smaller temple than the Parthenon, the Erechtheion, called after a legendary king of Athens, probably housed the wooden statue of Athena. Its famous porch has marble statues of women (*caryatids*) instead of columns, holding up the roof.

THE PARTHENON FRIEZE
The marble frieze of the Parthenon went around all four sides of the temple and was set up high, on the outside of the main building near the ceiling of the colonnade.

Its main subject was the procession of worshippers which wound its way up from the *agora* to the Acropolis every four years as a part of the festival called the Great Panathenaea in honour of the goddess Athena. Young men on horseback take up much of the frieze.

THE PARTHENON
The temple of the Parthenon occupies the highest point of the Acropolis. It was dedicated to Athena. The word Parthenon comes from the Greek word *parthenos* meaning virgin. Athena was sometimes described as Athena Parthenos. The Parthenon, which still stands today, was built between 447 and 432 B.C. The sculptures which decorated it were designed by Pheidias.

GOLDEN GODDESS
Inside the Parthenon stood a huge gold and ivory statue of the goddess Athena, made by the famous sculptor Pheidias, a close friend of Perikles. She appears in all her splendour as goddess of warfare. In this replica based on a smaller copy of the original statue and on descriptions by Greek writers, she wears her *aegis*, a small goatskin cloak fringed with snakes, and a high-crested helmet. On her right hand is a small winged figure of Nike, the goddess of victory.

An Athenian coin showing an owl, the bird of Athena

THE ELGIN MARBLES
Many of the sculptures from the Parthenon were brought to England by Lord Elgin, the British ambassador to the Ottoman court. He saw the sculptures when he visited Athens and was granted permission to bring some back to England. They can be seen today in the British Museum.

Temporary Elgin Room at the British Museum painted by A. Archer

Some young men are trotting gently along and others are galloping with their cloaks flying out behind them. The background to the frieze was originally painted, probably a bright blue. The horses used to have bridles of bronze.

The bridles have not survived, leaving only traces of the holes where they were attached to the marble. In the south frieze a number of young cows can be seen. In other parts of the frieze are women carrying sacrificial vessels, bowls, and jugs.

Power and politics in Athens

ANCIENT GREECE WAS MADE UP of a number of independent city-states. There were very few rich people and a great number of poor. In early times, the rich landowners and leaders called tyrants controlled the poor. In Athens and some other city-states the tyrants were driven out by the people, who acquired power and freedom. This new form of government was called democracy. It was invented in Athens. The Assembly was the main forum of political life. Meetings took place on a hill called the Pnyx near the Acropolis. Ordinary citizens, rich or poor, could make a speech and vote at the Assembly. At least 6,000 people had to be present for a meeting to take place. The Assembly made important decisions, for example, whether or not to declare war. A higher government body was a Council of 500 members, which arranged the business for the Assembly. It met in a round building called the *tholos.* In times of war, decisions were made about the defence of the city by a group of ten military commanders called *strategoi.* These were elected annually and could be re-elected many times.

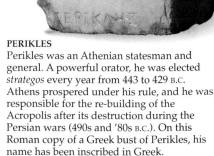

PERIKLES
Perikles was an Athenian statesman and general. A powerful orator, he was elected *strategos* every year from 443 to 429 B.C. Athens prospered under his rule, and he was responsible for the re-building of the Acropolis after its destruction during the Persian wars (490s and '80s B.C.). On this Roman copy of a Greek bust of Perikles, his name has been inscribed in Greek.

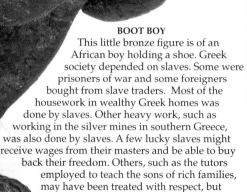

BOOT BOY
This little bronze figure is of an African boy holding a shoe. Greek society depended on slaves. Some were prisoners of war and some foreigners bought from slave traders. Most of the housework in wealthy Greek homes was done by slaves. Other heavy work, such as working in the silver mines in southern Greece, was also done by slaves. A few lucky slaves might receive wages from their masters and be able to buy back their freedom. Others, such as the tutors employed to teach the sons of rich families, may have been treated with respect, but most slaves probably led lives of drudgery.

PALACE OF WESTMINSTER
Many modern governments have been strongly influenced by the democratic system which developed in Athens in the fifth century B.C. The word democracy is Greek and it means "power of the people". It was not, however, a democracy as the term is used today, because a sizeable chunk of Greek society including women, foreigners, and slaves did not have the vote.

TREASURY OF TRIUMPH

The battle of Marathon was a famous victory by the Greeks over the Persians in 490 B.C. Soon afterwards this fine marble building was erected at Delphi by the Athenians as a symbol of triumph. It was a Treasury, full of Persian spoils, an expression of the prestige of Athens, and also a religious offering to Apollo at his holiest sanctuary. It stands in a prominent position beside the Sacred Way which winds up to the temple. This Treasury is a vivid illustration of the close links which existed between religion and politics in the ancient Greek world.

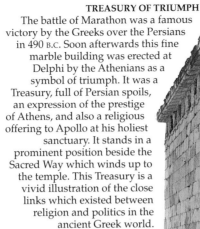

EXILE OF THEMISTOKLES

This coin shows an Athenian leader, Themistokles, whose main achievement was the creation of the fleet which enabled the Greeks to destroy the Persians at the battle of Salamis in 480 B.C. (pp. 54–55). Later, he was ostracised (banished) from Athens. When citizens wished to banish a politician, they would write his name on a piece of pot, an *ostrakon*, and these were counted. If more than 6,000 votes were cast he had to leave Athens for ten years.

WORDS OF BRONZE

This bronze tablet is inscribed with a treaty between the people of Elis and the citizens of Heraea in Arcadia in southern Greece. The treaty was to last 100 years, and the two parties promised to stand by one another, particularly in war. If either party failed to observe the treaty, there was a penalty of a talent of silver.

JUDGEMENT TABLET

This oblong tablet contains a treaty between the cities of Oeantheia and Chaleion. The two sides agreed that there should be a legal process for solving disputes about the ownership of land, and it imposed penalties should the treaty be broken by either side.

Gods, goddesses, and heroes

THE GREEKS BELIEVED that all the gods were descendants of Gaia (the earth) and Uranos (the sky). They thought the gods were probably very like humans: they fell in love with each other, married, quarrelled, had children, played music, and in many other ways mirrored human characteristics (or humans mirrored theirs). All the gods had their own spheres of influence. Demeter and Persephone were responsible for the grain growing, Artemis was the goddess of hunting, Apollo could foretell the future, and Aphrodite was the goddess of love. Many of the best-known gods had temples and sanctuaries dedicated to them, and much money and artistic ability were lavished upon them. Religion played a large part in the lives of ordinary people. Indeed, most of the beautiful buildings which still survive are temples. Worshippers believed that the gods would treat them well and meet their needs if they offered them the fruits of the harvest and animal sacrifices.

DIONYSOS FROM DELOS
Dionysos was the god of wine and earth fertility. In this mosaic from the island of Delos, he is riding a tiger.

THE KING OF THE GODS
Zeus was the king of the gods. He usually appears in art as a strong, middle-aged, bearded man, of great power and dignity. Sometimes he carries his symbol, a thunderbolt.

HOME OF THE GODS
Mount Olympus is the highest mountain in Greece and was believed to be the home of the gods. It is in the north of Greece, on the borders of Thessaly and Macedonia.

BEAUTY AND THE BEAST
On this mirror case, the goddess Aphrodite is playing a game of knucklebones (pp. 34–35) with the god Pan. The goddess of love and beauty is often shown by artists as a graceful, young woman with the upper part of her body bare. She is accompanied by Eros (according to some myths, her son), shown here as a small, winged boy, and also a goose, a symbol associated with her. Pan was a god of the countryside and had goat's legs and ears.

GODDESS OF LOVE
This bronze head of Aphrodite comes from eastern Turkey. The goddess was born from the sea foam and is thought to have been carried by the Zephyrs (West Winds) to Cyprus. Although she was married to Hephaistos, she fell in love with Ares, the god of war.

BRAIN CHILD
The strange birth of Athena was a favourite subject for Greek vase painters. She was the daughter of Zeus by the goddess Metis, meaning wisdom. Zeus was told that any child born to Metis would be more powerful than its father, and so, hoping to prevent this, he swallowed Metis. When the time came for Athena to be born, Zeus' head was cut open by the god Hephaistos and Athena emerged.

Apollo and Daphne by Italian artist Antonio del Pollaiuolo (1432–1498)

APOLLO AND DAPHNE
Daphne was a nymph loved by Apollo. According to one myth he tried to seize her, but she escaped. In answer to her prayer, Zeus turned her into a laurel tree, ironically, the tree sacred to Apollo.

HEPHAISTOS
The lame god Hephaistos, who was a smith, made a special axe to cut open Zeus' head. He also made a throne and shield for the king of the gods. He was the god of fire and husband of Aphrodite.

APOLLO
Apollo, a beautiful young deity, was the twin brother of Artemis, the goddess of the hunt. He had a famous shrine and oracle at Delphi. He is associated with the sun, with light, and with healing and medicine.

ATHENA
Athena was the patron goddess of the city of Athens. She was also the goddess of wisdom and warfare, and presided over the arts, literature, and philosophy. Her favourite bird was the owl and her favourite plant the olive tree, which she is credited with introducing to Athens. In the Trojan war (pp. 12–13) she fought on the side of the Greeks, and assisted Odysseus in his long voyage home.

DEMETER AND PERSEPHONE
Demeter and Persephone were mother and daughter and goddesses of the grain. This terracotta figure shows them sitting side-by-side wearing headdresses. They were probably holding the reins of an ox-cart which has not survived the years.

Continued on next page

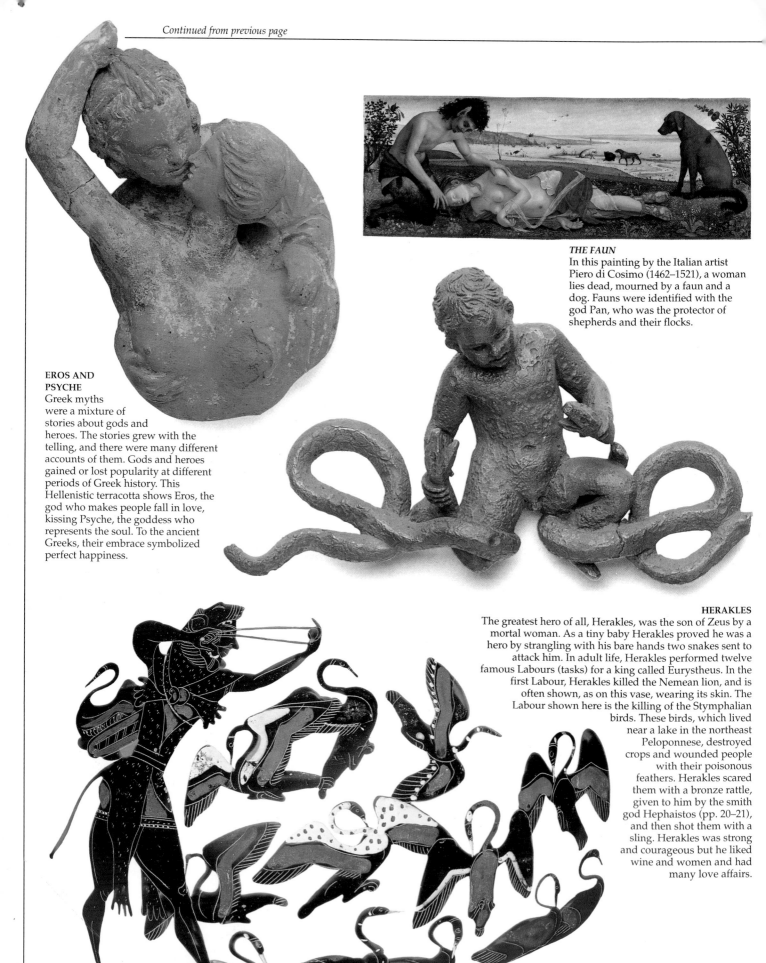

THE FAUN
In this painting by the Italian artist Piero di Cosimo (1462–1521), a woman lies dead, mourned by a faun and a dog. Fauns were identified with the god Pan, who was the protector of shepherds and their flocks.

EROS AND PSYCHE
Greek myths were a mixture of stories about gods and heroes. The stories grew with the telling, and there were many different accounts of them. Gods and heroes gained or lost popularity at different periods of Greek history. This Hellenistic terracotta shows Eros, the god who makes people fall in love, kissing Psyche, the goddess who represents the soul. To the ancient Greeks, their embrace symbolized perfect happiness.

HERAKLES
The greatest hero of all, Herakles, was the son of Zeus by a mortal woman. As a tiny baby Herakles proved he was a hero by strangling with his bare hands two snakes sent to attack him. In adult life, Herakles performed twelve famous Labours (tasks) for a king called Eurystheus. In the first Labour, Herakles killed the Nemean lion, and is often shown, as on this vase, wearing its skin. The Labour shown here is the killing of the Stymphalian birds. These birds, which lived near a lake in the northeast Peloponnese, destroyed crops and wounded people with their poisonous feathers. Herakles scared them with a bronze rattle, given to him by the smith god Hephaistos (pp. 20–21), and then shot them with a sling. Herakles was strong and courageous but he liked wine and women and had many love affairs.

THE BUILDING OF THE ARGO

This Roman terracotta wall panel shows a scene from the famous myth of Jason and the Argonauts. Jason was a prince from Thessaly in northern Greece and the Argonauts were a group of heroes who sailed with him on a ship they had built called the Argo. Heroes often battled with strange monsters, and often undertook long and difficult journeys. Jason and his crew set sail to find the Golden Fleece which hung on a tree near the Black Sea, guarded by a snake. The goddess Athena helped Jason in this task and she can be seen on the left helping the crew to construct the Argo.

PEGASUS

This coin shows the winged horse Pegasus. Pegasus was tamed by the hero Bellerophon who tried to ride him to heaven. But Pegasus was stung by a gadfly sent by Zeus and threw Bellerophon off his back and down to earth.

TOO HIGH!

Icarus was the son of Daedalus, a mythical craftsman who made wings for himself and his son, to enable them to fly. Their wings were attached by wax. Icarus flew too high, the heat of the sun melted the wax, and he fell into the Aegean Sea and drowned.

LURE OF THE LYRE

Orpheus was a poet and a musician. He played the lyre and the kithara and sang so well that he could tame wild animals; trees and plants would bend their branches to him, and he could soothe the most violent of tempers. He took part in the expedition of Jason and the Argonauts and calmed the crew and stilled the waves with his music. In this beautiful painting by Dutch painter Roelandt Savery (1576–1639), the magic of Orpheus' music is illustrated. All the birds and beasts are lying down together in an enchanted landscape.

PERSEUS AND MEDUSA

On this vase painting of 460 B.C., the hero Perseus has just cut off the head of the gorgon Medusa. One gaze from Medusa could turn a person to stone which is why Perseus beheaded her. Her head can be seen in Perseus' bag.

Festivals and oracles

COME DANCING
A row of people join hands and approach an altar where a sacrifice is blazing, at a festival in the countryside. A priestess, or perhaps Demeter, the corn goddess, stands behind the altar with a flat basket used for winnowing grain.

RELIGION PLAYED A MAJOR PART in Greek life. Greek worship centered around a small altar at home, usually in the courtyard of the house. The Greeks believed that they could strike a bargain with the gods. They offered them gold, silver, and animal sacrifice. They also held festivals and games in their honour. In return, they expected the gods to protect them from illness, look after their crops, and grant other favours. Communication with the gods had a regular place in the calendar; most festivals took place once a year, or sometimes every four years. Gods were also worshipped in sanctuaries – one of the most important was that of Apollo at Delphi. Apollo was well-known as a god of prophecy, and at Delphi he would reply to questions about the future. His priestess would act as the mouthpiece of the god and make obscure pronouncements which could be interpreted in different ways. The oracle (as these forecasts were called) at Delphi, lasted into Christian times.

HOLY BULL
A bull was one of the animals offered at important sacrificial occasions. Bulls would be decorated with garlands of plants and ribbons to show that they had been set aside for the gods. Garlanded bulls' heads were the inspiration for some of the decorative patterns on temples.

SOMETHING OLD, SOMETHING NEW
The huge columns of a Greek temple at ancient Poseidonia (Paestum) in southern Italy frame a bride and groom posing for their wedding photos. Ancient ruins like these are believed to bring good luck to a new marriage.

CENTRE OF THE WORLD
Delphi was thought to be the centre of the world, at the very point where two birds flying from opposite ends of the earth met. The Greeks placed a huge stone there, the *omphalos*, or navel of the world. Carved on this version, which is in the museum at Delphi, is a network of woollen strands. These were a sign that this was a holy object.

THE CHARIOTEER
A stadium was built high above the temple to Apollo at Delphi, for games and chariot races in honour of the god. Winning the chariot race was the greatest honour of the games, and the owner of the winning team of horses paid for a statue to celebrate his success. The eyes of this magnificent bronze statue are inlaid with glass and stone, the lips are copper, and the headband is patterned with silver. The charioteer is still holding the reins of his horses even though they have long disappeared. This is perhaps one of the best-known statues of ancient Greece.

TEMPLE OF APOLLO
Delphi was the home of the main shrine of Apollo. It lies on the steep slopes of Mount Parnassus, the favourite haunt of Apollo and also of the Muses who looked after arts and music. A road lined with small buildings to house the rich gifts made to the god, still winds its way up the slope and past the remains of his great temple which housed the oracle.

SANCTUARY OF ATHENA
The sanctuary of Athena lies further down the mountain from Apollo's shrine. In the middle of it is this circular building, the purpose of which is unknown. It is set against the silvery blue background of thousands of olive trees. Athena was supposed to have created the olive tree, and these groves still provide a rich harvest for local people.

THE WAY TO ATHENA
In the goddess Athena's own city of Athens lay the Panathenaic Way, a special road that led up to her temples and altars on the Acropolis. Leading up from the *agora*, the market and meeting place of the city, the road today passes the rebuilt version of a *stoa*, a long, colonnaded building. It was used for commerce and conversation.

PROCESSION OF SACRIFICE
On this broad bowl used for wine (the ivy leaves which decorate it are linked with Dionysos, the wine god), a long line of people are on their way to worship the goddess Athena. The altar where the flames are already rising is on the right of the bowl. Athena is standing behind the altar. The procession is led by a woman carrying a tray of cakes on her head. She is followed by a man leading the sacrificial bull, then a man playing the double pipes. The rest of the men in the procession carry all the objects necessary for the worship of the goddess, such as a jug of wine. A mule cart brings up the rear.

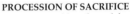

Temples

GREEK LIFE WAS DOMINATED by religion and so it is not surprising that the temples of ancient Greece were the biggest and most beautiful buildings. They also had a political purpose as they were often built to celebrate civic power and pride, or to offer thanksgiving to the patron deity of a city for success in war. Temples were made of limestone or marble with roofs and ceilings of wood. Roof tiles were made of terracotta or stone. Large numbers of workers must have been employed in temple construction. Huge stone blocks had to be transported from quarries in ox-drawn carts. These blocks were carved on site by masons using hammers and mallets. The tall columns were made in cylindrical sections ("drums"), lifted into position with ropes and pulleys, and held together with pegs. Decorative sculpture in the form of friezes, and statues in the pediments (the triangular gable ends), added to the grandeur and beauty of Greek temples.

CAPE SOUNION
A fifth-century marble temple to Poseidon, god of the sea, crowns a high promontory south of Athens. It was a landmark for sailors returning home to Athens. The English romantic poet Lord Byron (1788–1824) was very moved by its beauty.

ZEUS' TEMPLE
A great international festival of athletics (pp. 44–45) in honour of Zeus was held every four years at Olympia, a sanctuary on the banks of the river Alpheios. Colossal remains of the great temple of Zeus built in the fifth century, and other important buildings, have been found there.

TEMPLE OF CERES
Poseidonia (later called Paestum) in southern Italy, south of Naples, was a rich Greek colony and it has the best preserved archaic temples anywhere in the Greek world. This one, built in the sixth century B.C. in the Doric style and known as the temple of Ceres (the Roman version of Demeter), was in fact dedicated to the goddess Athena and later used as a Christian church. For hundreds of years few people visited the site of Paestum because it was hidden by swamps and undergrowth, and this accounts for the remarkable survival of the buildings.

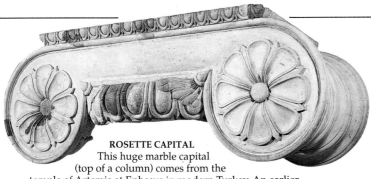

ROSETTE CAPITAL
This huge marble capital (top of a column) comes from the temple of Artemis at Ephesus in modern Turkey. An earlier temple on the same site was destroyed by fire in 356 B.C., on the same night that Alexander the Great (pp. 62–63) was born.

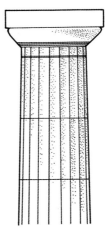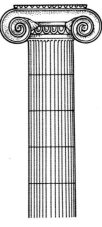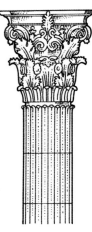

DORIC
The Doric style is rather sturdy and its top (the capital), is plain. This style was used in mainland Greece and the colonies in southern Italy and Sicily.

IONIC
The Ionic style is thinner and more elegant. Its capital is decorated with a scroll-like design (a volute). This style was found in eastern Greece and the islands.

CORINTHIAN
The Corinthian style is seldom used in the Greek world, but often seen on Roman temples. Its capital is very elaborate and decorated with acanthus leaves.

LION'S MOUTH
Rain water was sometimes drained away from the roofs of temples through spouts in the form of lions' heads. This one comes from a temple of Athena at Priene, just south of Ephesus, in modern Turkey.

COLUMNS AND CAPITALS
Most Greek buildings had vertical columns and horizontal lintels (beams). This style of construction may have been inspired by earlier wooden buildings whose roofs were supported by tree trunks.

CORINTHIAN CAPITAL
This Corinthian capital once decorated a gracious colonnaded building in Asia Minor (modern Turkey). The face is a version of a female theatrical mask. The deeply carved leaves below copy those of the acanthus plant, a favourite motif of Greek artists. The plant is easily identified by its spreading, leathery leaves.

PALMETTE ROOF TILE
The end of this roof tile is decorated with a palmette shape. It comes from a temple to Apollo at Bassae in southern Greece. This area was famous for its fighting men and Apollo may have been worshipped here as a god of soldiers.

LOTUS LEAVES
This marble fragment is crisply carved with a frieze of lotus and palmette designs and other delicate mouldings. It comes from the top part of the east wall of the famous temple of the Erechtheion on the Acropolis of Athens (pp. 16–17). The roof of the south porch of the building is supported by columns in the form of standing women with baskets on their heads. Perikles ordered the construction of the Erechtheion (which survives today on the site of older buildings) in the mid fifth century B.C. to beautify the city of Athens.

At home

THE GREEKS LIKED THEIR HOMES to be private. The windows were small and set high in the walls, which were made out of sun-dried mud bricks and did not survive well. This farmhouse is a fairly simple building and town houses would probably have had more rooms and been more luxurious. The garden or courtyard was in the middle of the house with all the rooms arranged around it. There might be a well here where slave girls did the family washing and filled the water pots. In the porch, a *herm*, a statue of the god Hermes, prevented evil spirits from entering. It is difficult to get a very clear picture of a typical Greek home. This farmhouse is based on information gathered from excavating a house in the country to the south of Athens, which was occupied in the fourth century B.C.

Terracotta figurine shows a woman grinding grain to make bread

DOORS AND JARS
Wood was expensive in Greece and doors were therefore precious objects. Two bowls on stands used in wedding rituals can be seen in front.

RAIN CAT
Some rich houses had gutters on the roofs for the removal of rain water. The water flowed onto the ground through water spouts like this attractive one shaped like a lion's head.

The women's quarters (gynaeceum) housed the weaving looms, babies' cradles, and couches

Ladder to upper storey

Every house had an altar where the family would offer sacrifices to the gods

Hearth for cooking and to provide burning charcoal for portable braziers

The dining room (andron) where the men entertained their friends

SITTING PRETTY
In this vase painting, a young woman, perhaps a bride preparing for her wedding, is sitting on a chair in her house. This elegant shape of chair is often seen on vases.

COUCHES
As Greek couches were made mainly of wood, none have survived. This bronze decoration was once fitted onto a couch near the head rest. Similar couches were used at meal times.

ON THE TILES
Sometimes the ends of terracotta roof tiles in wealthier homes and in temples were decorated with human and animal faces. This gorgon head has tight curls and a protuding tongue. Originally it would have been brightly coloured and clearly visible from the ground.

Roof made of clay tiles

Walls made of mud bricks, sometimes plastered over

Window openings without glass but with wooden shutters

Wooden door with bronze fittings

Porch pillars made from fallen or cut down trees on the farm land

Stone foundations were often stolen by later builders

In the country a stone wall usually surrounded the property

Women's world

Whorl

THE LIVES OF WOMEN in ancient Greece were restricted. They were very much under the control of their husbands, fathers, or brothers, and rarely took part in politics or any form of public life. Most women could not inherit property and were allowed very little money. A girl would marry very young, at the age of 13 or 14, and her husband, who was certain to be much older, was chosen for her by her father. The main purpose of marriage was to have a baby, preferably a boy, to carry on the male line. The status of a woman greatly increased when she had given birth to a boy (pp. 32–33). Some marriages seem to have been happy. A number of tombstones have survived that commemorate women who had died in childbirth. There are tender inscriptions from the grieving husbands. It is possible that, although legally they had very little freedom, some women could make important decisions about family life. Their spinning and weaving work also made an important contribution to the household.

Greek Woman by British artist Sir Lawrence Alma-Tadema (1836–1912)

HOME MAKERS
Girls in Greece did not go to school (pp. 32–33). Instead, they stayed at home and were taught by their mothers how to spin and weave and look after the house. Some wealthier women might be taught to read and write. On this vase a woman is reading from a papyrus scroll.

SPINDLE
Wool was spun into yarn with a spindle. This one is made of wood, but bronze and bone examples also exist. At one end is a weight, known as a spindle whorl. The spindle twirls around and spins the wool fibre into thread.

SPINNER
On this white-ground jug a woman is spinning with both a distaff and spindle. The distaff was a shaft of wood or metal with a spike at one end and a handle at the other.

WELL WOMEN
In Athens there were public fountains where women and slave girls went to fill their water pots. Not many houses had their own private wells. The water spout is in the shape of a lion's head. The women stand waiting their turn with their water pots balanced on their heads. This was a good opportunity to meet with friends and chat.

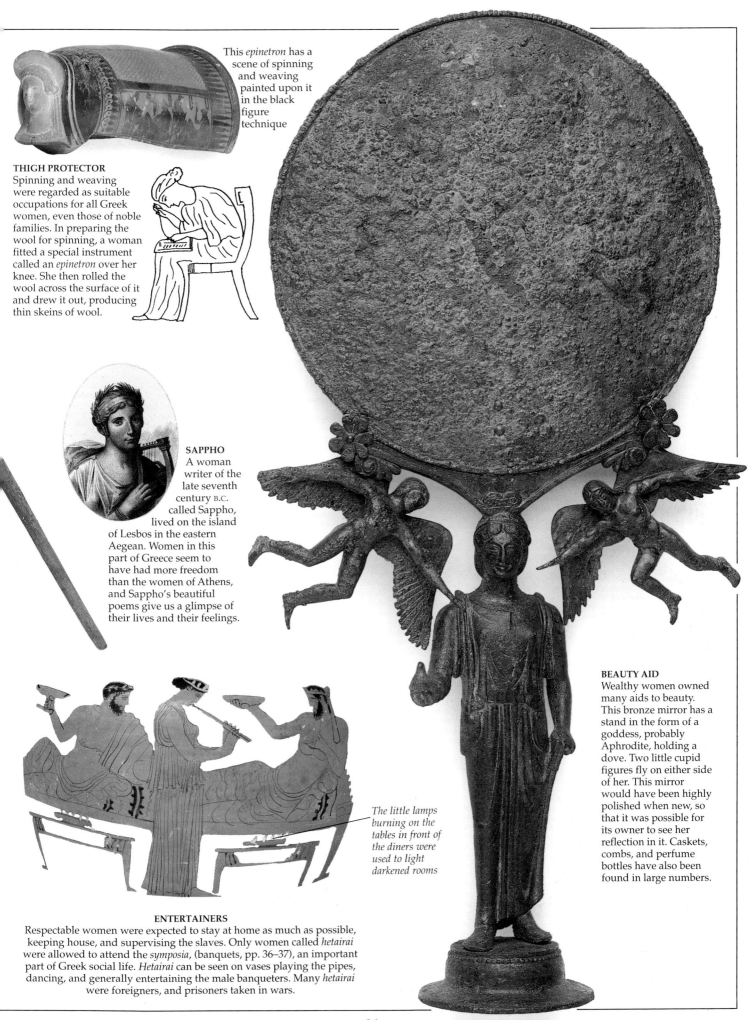

This *epinetron* has a scene of spinning and weaving painted upon it in the black figure technique

THIGH PROTECTOR
Spinning and weaving were regarded as suitable occupations for all Greek women, even those of noble families. In preparing the wool for spinning, a woman fitted a special instrument called an *epinetron* over her knee. She then rolled the wool across the surface of it and drew it out, producing thin skeins of wool.

SAPPHO
A woman writer of the late seventh century B.C. called Sappho, lived on the island of Lesbos in the eastern Aegean. Women in this part of Greece seem to have had more freedom than the women of Athens, and Sappho's beautiful poems give us a glimpse of their lives and their feelings.

BEAUTY AID
Wealthy women owned many aids to beauty. This bronze mirror has a stand in the form of a goddess, probably Aphrodite, holding a dove. Two little cupid figures fly on either side of her. This mirror would have been highly polished when new, so that it was possible for its owner to see her reflection in it. Caskets, combs, and perfume bottles have also been found in large numbers.

The little lamps burning on the tables in front of the diners were used to light darkened rooms

ENTERTAINERS
Respectable women were expected to stay at home as much as possible, keeping house, and supervising the slaves. Only women called *hetairai* were allowed to attend the *symposia*, (banquets, pp. 36–37), an important part of Greek social life. *Hetairai* can be seen on vases playing the pipes, dancing, and generally entertaining the male banqueters. Many *hetairai* were foreigners, and prisoners taken in wars.

31

Growing up in Greece

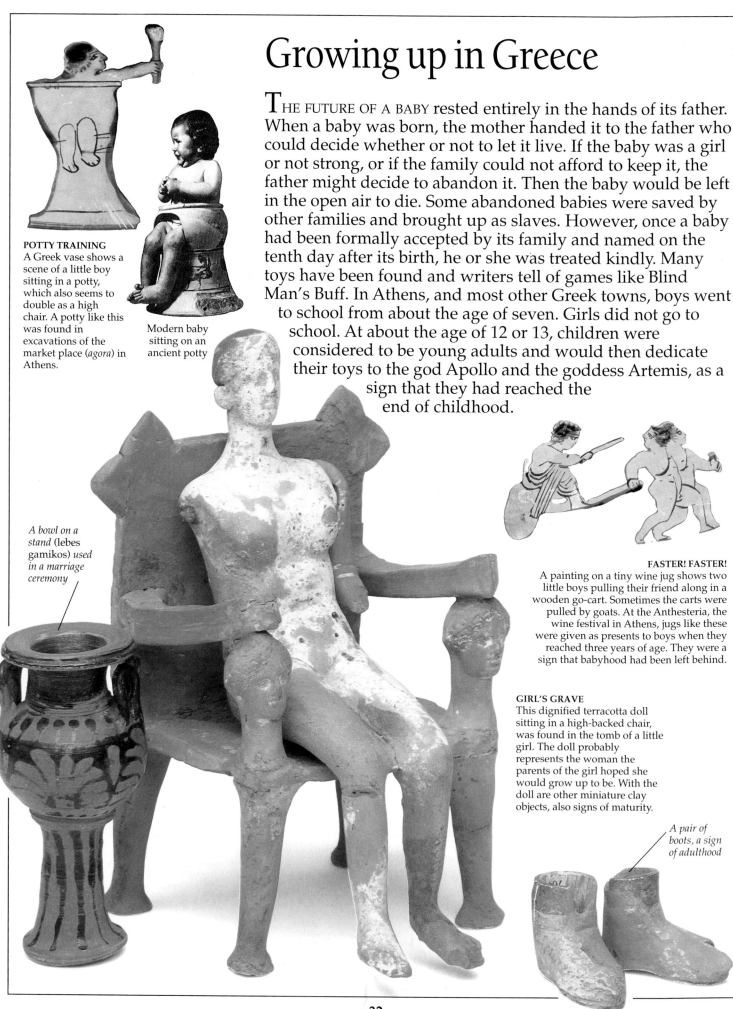

The future of a baby rested entirely in the hands of its father. When a baby was born, the mother handed it to the father who could decide whether or not to let it live. If the baby was a girl or not strong, or if the family could not afford to keep it, the father might decide to abandon it. Then the baby would be left in the open air to die. Some abandoned babies were saved by other families and brought up as slaves. However, once a baby had been formally accepted by its family and named on the tenth day after its birth, he or she was treated kindly. Many toys have been found and writers tell of games like Blind Man's Buff. In Athens, and most other Greek towns, boys went to school from about the age of seven. Girls did not go to school. At about the age of 12 or 13, children were considered to be young adults and would then dedicate their toys to the god Apollo and the goddess Artemis, as a sign that they had reached the end of childhood.

POTTY TRAINING
A Greek vase shows a scene of a little boy sitting in a potty, which also seems to double as a high chair. A potty like this was found in excavations of the market place (*agora*) in Athens.

Modern baby sitting on an ancient potty

A bowl on a stand (lebes gamikos) *used in a marriage ceremony*

FASTER! FASTER!
A painting on a tiny wine jug shows two little boys pulling their friend along in a wooden go-cart. Sometimes the carts were pulled by goats. At the Anthesteria, the wine festival in Athens, jugs like these were given as presents to boys when they reached three years of age. They were a sign that babyhood had been left behind.

GIRL'S GRAVE
This dignified terracotta doll sitting in a high-backed chair, was found in the tomb of a little girl. The doll probably represents the woman the parents of the girl hoped she would grow up to be. With the doll are other miniature clay objects, also signs of maturity.

A pair of boots, a sign of adulthood

Education

When boys went to school at seven, they learned reading, writing, and arithmetic from a teacher called a *grammatistes*. They learned music, including the playing of a musical instrument, from a teacher known as a *kitharistes*. They also had to learn poetry by heart and the art of debating. Older boys might be taught by teachers called Sophists. Sophists travelled from town to town and often taught their students in the *gymnasia*, or training grounds. Although girls did not go to school, some girls from well-off families had private tutors and they too learned to read and write. Their mothers taught them spinning and weaving, and how to run a home.

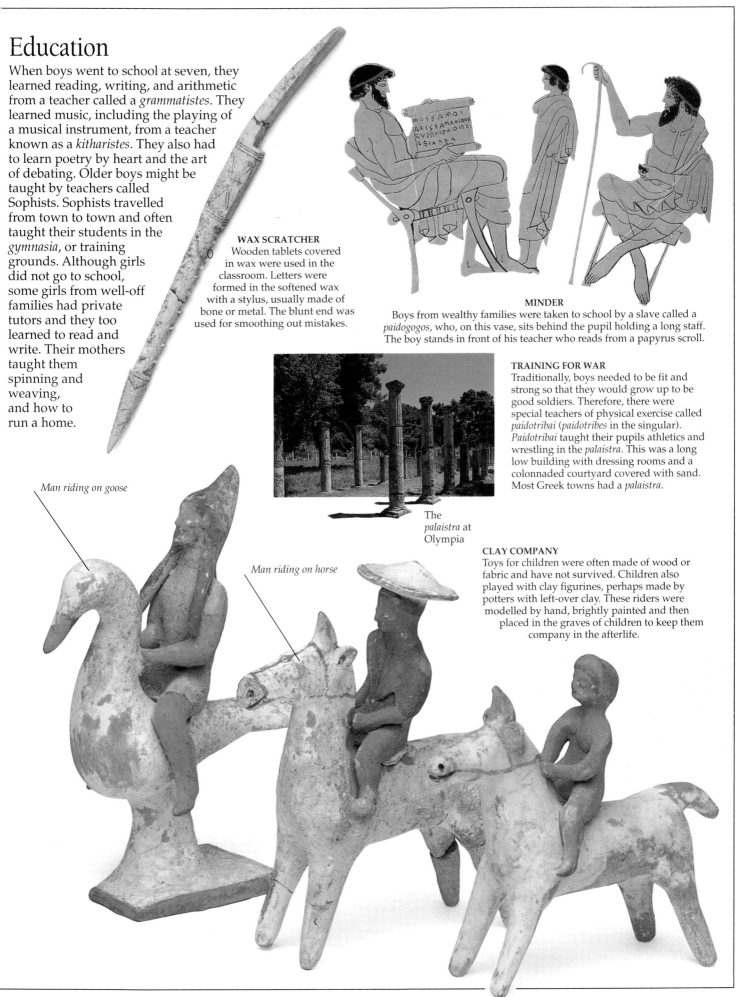

WAX SCRATCHER
Wooden tablets covered in wax were used in the classroom. Letters were formed in the softened wax with a stylus, usually made of bone or metal. The blunt end was used for smoothing out mistakes.

MINDER
Boys from wealthy families were taken to school by a slave called a *paidogogos*, who, on this vase, sits behind the pupil holding a long staff. The boy stands in front of his teacher who reads from a papyrus scroll.

TRAINING FOR WAR
Traditionally, boys needed to be fit and strong so that they would grow up to be good soldiers. Therefore, there were special teachers of physical exercise called *paidotribai* (*paidotribes* in the singular). *Paidotribai* taught their pupils athletics and wrestling in the *palaistra*. This was a long low building with dressing rooms and a colonnaded courtyard covered with sand. Most Greek towns had a *palaistra*.

The *palaistra* at Olympia

CLAY COMPANY
Toys for children were often made of wood or fabric and have not survived. Children also played with clay figurines, perhaps made by potters with left-over clay. These riders were modelled by hand, brightly painted and then placed in the graves of children to keep them company in the afterlife.

Man riding on goose

Man riding on horse

Fun and games

Rich Greeks, especially those who lived in towns, had plenty of leisure time to spend talking, giving dinner parties, visiting the gymnasium, and playing all kinds of games. Music was particularly important. Greeks sang songs at births, weddings, and funerals. They had love songs, battle songs, drinking songs, and songs of thanksgiving to the gods to celebrate the harvest. There were also many musical instruments: stringed instruments like the harp, the lyre, and the kithara (a kind of lyre), and wind instruments like the syrinx, or pan pipes, made of reeds of different lengths. Unfortunately, almost no written music has survived from ancient Greece. Perhaps we can guess what it may have sounded like by seeing the way women dance on Greek vases. They seem to be moving rhythmically to slow and haunting tunes. Greek men did not dance, but they liked to watch dancers perform at celebrations and at drinking parties (pp. 36–37). Poor Greeks, such as farmers and slaves, had very little spare time.

DANCING GIRL
This slave girl, wearing a short, pleated skirt, is dancing while playing the castanets. She is probably an entertainer at a party.

CLASH OF CYMBALS
This pair of bronze cymbals is inscribed with their owner's name, Oata. Musical instruments like this have survived very rarely, although they can often be seen on vase paintings.

TUNEFUL TRIO
This painting from a red figure vase, shows three people with their musical instruments. The woman sitting on the chair is the Muse Terpsichore. Muses were minor deities who looked after all the arts. Terpsichore seems to be concentrating hard on playing her harp, while the other two hold their lyres and listen. The man on the right is Musaios, a legendary musician.

Knucklebones

LARGE LYRE
The kithara, which this woman is playing, is a larger, wooden version of the lyre. She is plucking the strings with a plectrum, similar to those used by guitarists today. The kithara was usually played by professional musicians. This figure was made in a Greek town in southern Italy. Perhaps she is singing or chanting poetry while she plays.

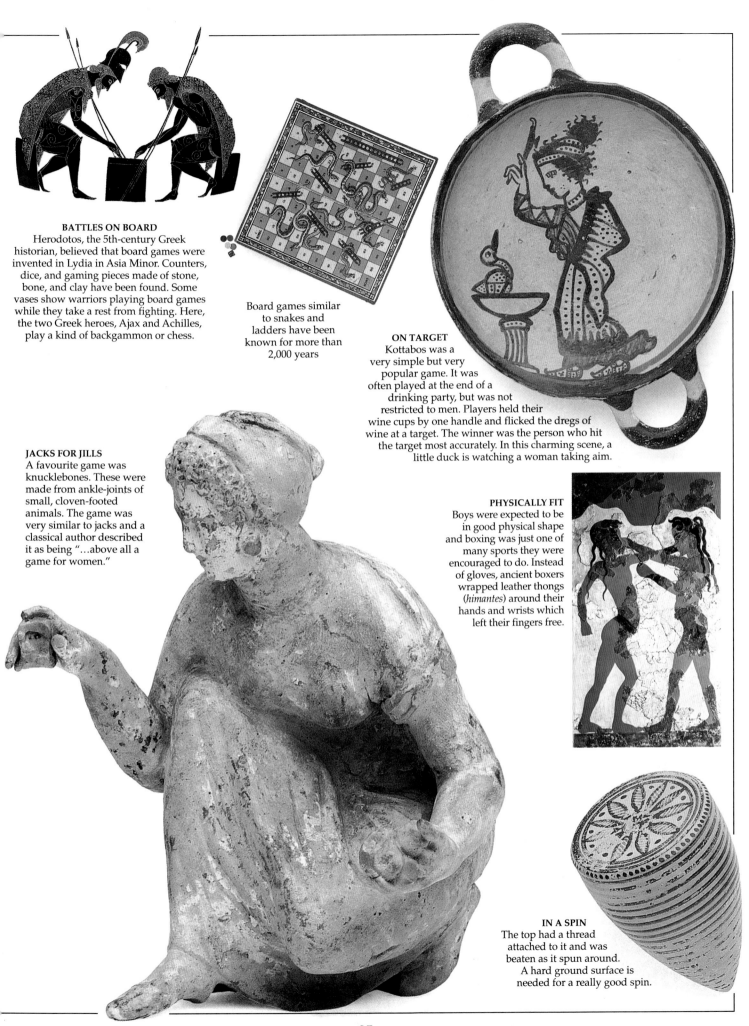

BATTLES ON BOARD
Herodotos, the 5th-century Greek historian, believed that board games were invented in Lydia in Asia Minor. Counters, dice, and gaming pieces made of stone, bone, and clay have been found. Some vases show warriors playing board games while they take a rest from fighting. Here, the two Greek heroes, Ajax and Achilles, play a kind of backgammon or chess.

Board games similar to snakes and ladders have been known for more than 2,000 years

ON TARGET
Kottabos was a very simple but very popular game. It was often played at the end of a drinking party, but was not restricted to men. Players held their wine cups by one handle and flicked the dregs of wine at a target. The winner was the person who hit the target most accurately. In this charming scene, a little duck is watching a woman taking aim.

JACKS FOR JILLS
A favourite game was knucklebones. These were made from ankle-joints of small, cloven-footed animals. The game was very similar to jacks and a classical author described it as being "…above all a game for women."

PHYSICALLY FIT
Boys were expected to be in good physical shape and boxing was just one of many sports they were encouraged to do. Instead of gloves, ancient boxers wrapped leather thongs (*himantes*) around their hands and wrists which left their fingers free.

IN A SPIN
The top had a thread attached to it and was beaten as it spun around. A hard ground surface is needed for a really good spin.

Wining and dining

IN ATHENS, AND OTHER GREEK CITIES, men often held banquets or drinking parties (*symposia*), for their male friends. As well as these smaller, private *symposia*, there were also large-scale public ones. Private *symposia* took place at home in the dining room (*andron*) which was set aside for the men's use after the evening meal. Many Greek vases show *symposia* scenes. All respectable women were excluded from a *symposion*, but slave girls called *hetairai* would entertain the men with their dancing, flute playing, and acrobatic displays (pp. 30–31). The evening began with the pouring of libations (usually wine), and the singing of special songs or hymns, to the gods. The guests wore garlands and perfume. Early in the evening they might discuss politics and philosophy, but as they drank more and more wine, they would tell each other jokes, riddles, and stories. Eventually, after drinking a great deal of wine, the banqueters would fall asleep on their comfortable couches, leaving the women and slave boys to tidy up.

DRINKING CUP
This is a special kind of drinking cup used at a *symposion*. It is in the form of a ram's head and the rim is painted with a banqueting scene of guests leaning back on cushioned couches. It gives us a clear impression of the elegant and comfortable lifestyle which wealthy Athenian men enjoyed. The cup has no base so was probably passed round from hand to hand.

Olives are plentiful in Greece and bowls of olives, both green and black, would be offered at a *symposion* possibly as an appetizer

WINE VESSELS
Wine was the Greeks' favourite drink. It was drunk by everybody, not just the rich, and was nearly always diluted with water. Bread dipped in wine, eaten with a few figs, was a typical Greek breakfast. Many different kinds of wine container have survived. These are often made of clay, but sometimes of bronze. The big, bronze vessel on the far left was used for mixing water and wine together. The mixture would then have been transferred to the jug with the ladle and the slave would fill his master's cup.

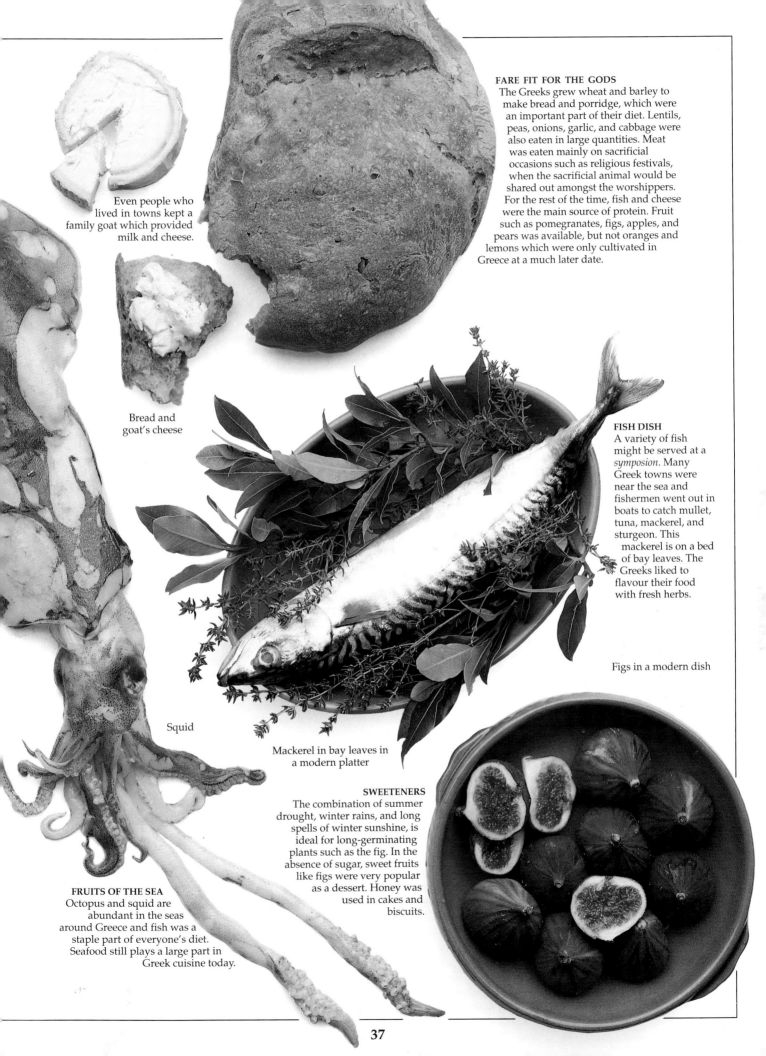

Even people who lived in towns kept a family goat which provided milk and cheese.

Bread and goat's cheese

FARE FIT FOR THE GODS

The Greeks grew wheat and barley to make bread and porridge, which were an important part of their diet. Lentils, peas, onions, garlic, and cabbage were also eaten in large quantities. Meat was eaten mainly on sacrificial occasions such as religious festivals, when the sacrificial animal would be shared out amongst the worshippers. For the rest of the time, fish and cheese were the main source of protein. Fruit such as pomegranates, figs, apples, and pears was available, but not oranges and lemons which were only cultivated in Greece at a much later date.

FISH DISH

A variety of fish might be served at a *symposion*. Many Greek towns were near the sea and fishermen went out in boats to catch mullet, tuna, mackerel, and sturgeon. This mackerel is on a bed of bay leaves. The Greeks liked to flavour their food with fresh herbs.

Squid

Figs in a modern dish

Mackerel in bay leaves in a modern platter

SWEETENERS

The combination of summer drought, winter rains, and long spells of winter sunshine, is ideal for long-germinating plants such as the fig. In the absence of sugar, sweet fruits like figs were very popular as a dessert. Honey was used in cakes and biscuits.

FRUITS OF THE SEA

Octopus and squid are abundant in the seas around Greece and fish was a staple part of everyone's diet. Seafood still plays a large part in Greek cuisine today.

A day out

GREEK THEATRES ARE AMONG the most spectacular buildings that survive from ancient times. In cities like Athens, or at sacred sites like Delphi and Epidauros, people flocked to see dramas in honour of the gods. In Athens, performances for the wine god Dionysos developed into what are now known as plays. From the middle of the sixth century B.C., plays, organized as dramatic competitions, were put on during the spring festival of Dionysos. By the fifth century B.C., both tragedies and comedies were performed and many have survived to the present time. Audiences in Athens spent days watching the plays, seated in the theatre of Dionysos on the slope of the Acropolis. The actors were all men, even taking the female parts, and no more than three main actors could speak to each other at one time. A larger group of actors, the chorus, commented on the play's action and addressed the audience more directly. Music accompanied the plays, which were acted out on a flat circular area called the *orchestra*. Women were probably not allowed to go to the theatre at all.

EURIPIDES
The expression on this sculpture reflects the serious subjects dealt with by the Athenian playwright Euripides. Some of his plays dealt with the horrors of war, and upset the Athenians because they hinted at Athens' savage treatment of her enemies.

TIRED OUT
This small terracotta figure shows a comic actor dressed as an old woman. He wears a mask with a wrinkled face and crinkly hair which he has pushed back on his head, as he rests wearily on a seat.

BIRD'S EYE VIEW
From high up in the back row at Epidauros you can get a clear view of the performance. Here, a temporary set has been built for the modern production of a play.

EPIDAUROS
This ground-level view of the 14,000 seat theatre at Epidauros, gives an idea of what it is like to be an actor going into the performing area. The carefully curved auditorium (*theatron* or viewing theatre) is a huge semi-circular bowl cut into the surface of the hillside. Its shape is not just designed for excellent viewing; sound, too, is caught and amplified, and actors speaking in the *orchestra* can be heard in the back row.

GREEK DRAMA ALIVE AND WELL
A group of actors from Britain's Royal National Theatre perform three plays called *The Oresteia*, by the Athenian playwright Aeschylus. They tell of the death of Agamemnon after the Trojan war and how his son Orestes avenged him.

SOPHOKLES
Portraits of famous playwrights were produced some time after their death, so they were not true likenesses. But these sculptures honoured the memory of great writers like the playwright Sophokles. This print decorates a 19th-century text of the plays. Sophokles' plays about royal or legendary families and their tragic lives, like those of King Oedipus or Electra daughter of Agamemnon, still grip audiences today.

The very elaborate hat is a sign that this bearded man's wealth was not acquired honestly

The muse holds a mask portraying a young woman, one of the characters in Greek comedy from the fourth century B.C.

SOUVENIR STATUETTES
Statuettes in terracotta, originally painted in bright colours, are perhaps souvenirs of theatre visits. Also, sets of the entire casts of plays have been found in graves. The graceful female figure is probably a muse, one of the nine guardians of the arts in Greek mythology. The terracotta of the bearded actor represents a sinister figure from later Greek comedy, who lived off the earnings of *hetairai*.

Body beautiful

BEAUTY AND CLEANLINESS were important to the ancient Greeks. In sculpture and on vases, both men and women can be seen wearing elegant, softly-folded garments and standing in graceful poses (pp. 42–43). Young men took great care of their bodies, keeping them fit and strong so that they could be good soldiers and athletes. Nudity was considered quite normal for young men who always competed naked at their Games (pp. 44–45). After exercise, men and boys rubbed themselves with olive oil to keep their skins supple. Women had their whole bodies clothed, including their heads when they went out. Their clothes were so finely spun, however, that they were sometimes almost transparent, and must have been light and cool to wear in the hot summer. Women wore perfumed oils and tried to keep out of the sun as much as possible, because a sun tan was not considered beautiful. Wealthy women owned jewellery, much of it in gold and silver and very ornate.

THE AEGINA TREASURE
This gold earring is one of a pair that was found, with a pendant, on the island of Aegina. It was made in Minoan times (pp. 8–9). The circular shape is a snake, and inside it are two dogs standing on the heads of monkeys.

DECORATION IN DEATH
Jewellery was an indication of wealth and prosperity. On this grave relief, a slave is shown handing a bracelet to a woman, probably the dead person herself.

FOLLOWER OF FASHION
This terracotta figurine shows a fashionable Greek woman (pp. 42–43) wearing a tunic (*chiton*) and cloak (*himation*). She is holding a kind of fan. Clothes were often brightly coloured as can be seen from the traces of paint which remain on the statuette. Hairstyles were very elaborate and this woman is wearing some kind of head decoration. Many figures like this have been found at Tanagra in central Greece.

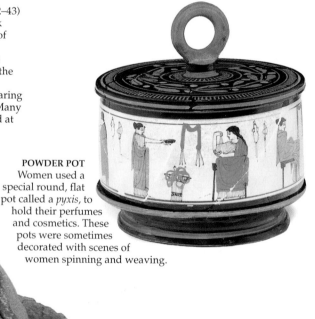

POWDER POT
Women used a special round, flat pot called a *pyxis*, to hold their perfumes and cosmetics. These pots were sometimes decorated with scenes of women spinning and weaving.

BATH TIME
Greeks bathed very regularly. This terracotta shows that baths were smaller than most modern ones. At the feet end of this bath, there was a hollow where the water was deeper so that the woman could splash it backwards over her body.

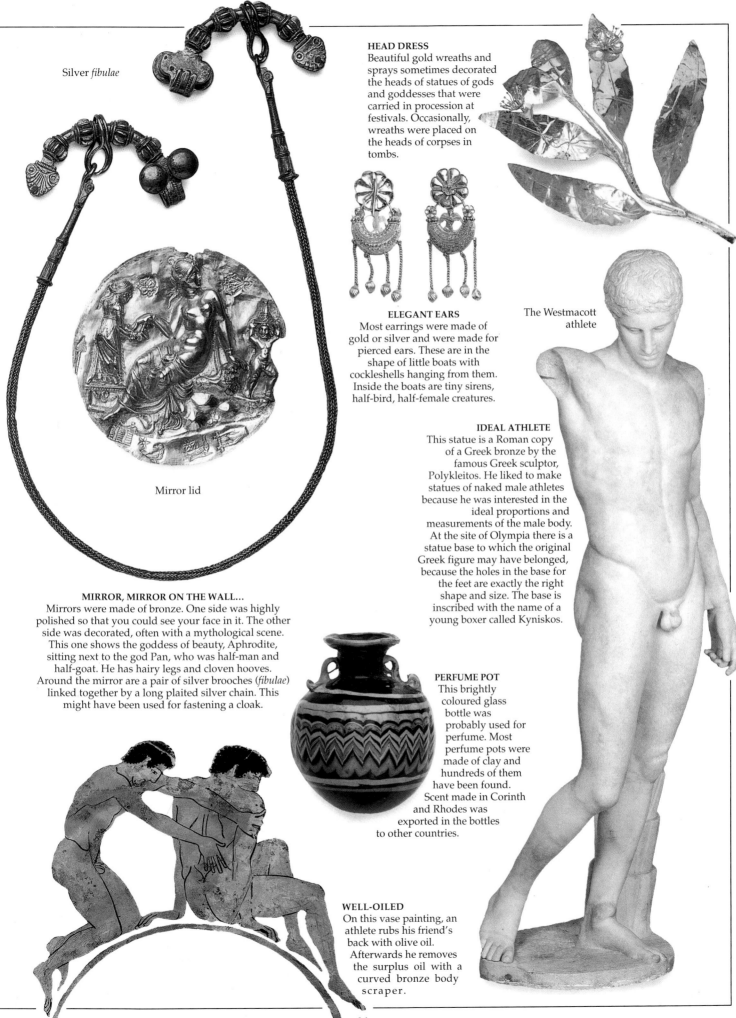

Silver *fibulae*

Mirror lid

HEAD DRESS
Beautiful gold wreaths and sprays sometimes decorated the heads of statues of gods and goddesses that were carried in procession at festivals. Occasionally, wreaths were placed on the heads of corpses in tombs.

ELEGANT EARS
Most earrings were made of gold or silver and were made for pierced ears. These are in the shape of little boats with cockleshells hanging from them. Inside the boats are tiny sirens, half-bird, half-female creatures.

The Westmacott athlete

IDEAL ATHLETE
This statue is a Roman copy of a Greek bronze by the famous Greek sculptor, Polykleitos. He liked to make statues of naked male athletes because he was interested in the ideal proportions and measurements of the male body. At the site of Olympia there is a statue base to which the original Greek figure may have belonged, because the holes in the base for the feet are exactly the right shape and size. The base is inscribed with the name of a young boxer called Kyniskos.

MIRROR, MIRROR ON THE WALL...
Mirrors were made of bronze. One side was highly polished so that you could see your face in it. The other side was decorated, often with a mythological scene. This one shows the goddess of beauty, Aphrodite, sitting next to the god Pan, who was half-man and half-goat. He has hairy legs and cloven hooves. Around the mirror are a pair of silver brooches (*fibulae*) linked together by a long plaited silver chain. This might have been used for fastening a cloak.

PERFUME POT
This brightly coloured glass bottle was probably used for perfume. Most perfume pots were made of clay and hundreds of them have been found. Scent made in Corinth and Rhodes was exported in the bottles to other countries.

WELL-OILED
On this vase painting, an athlete rubs his friend's back with olive oil. Afterwards he removes the surplus oil with a curved bronze body scraper.

Clothes for comfort

GREEK CLOTHES WERE MADE largely of wool provided by local sheep. The wool was spun very finely so that garments were thinner than modern woollen clothing. Lighter linen clothes made out of spun flax were also worn. Very wealthy people bought expensive silks from the East, and in Hellenistic times, mulberry trees were planted on the island of Kos to provide a home-grown silk industry. Bright colours were popular especially among women. Purple was obtained from sea snails and a violet shade from a scaly insect larva called the kermes worm. Other dyes came from plants. Poorer people probably wore undyed clothes. The shapes of clothes were much the same for both men and women and hardly changed over hundreds of years. The basic dress was a straight tunic fastened at the shoulder with brooches or pins and with a cloak flung over the top.

LADY HAMILTON
Sir William Hamilton, British Ambassador to Naples in the late 18th century, was a collector of Greek antiquities. His wife Emma, famous for her liaison with Lord Nelson, often dressed in Greek costume.

HAIR DRESSING
Greek women (except slave women) wore their hair long. This woman's style was fashionable in the Classical period. The hair is piled up at the back of the head and held in place with a net and ribbons. Diadems, and other gold hair decorations, were worn on special occasions.

READY TO WEAR
The *chiton* was said to have been invented in the Greek colony of Ionia. It was made from a single rectangle of cloth, cut into two and fastened at intervals from neck to elbows to give a graceful loose sleeve effect. It was gathered at the waist with a belt. The *chiton* shown here is made out of modern woollen fabric. This is perhaps slightly thicker and fuller than the original material would have been in the fifth century B.C. Another earlier kind of *chiton*, sometimes called a *peplos*, originated in mainland Greece. It was secured with big pins on the shoulders and did not have sleeves.

Chiton

WRAP UP
Greek underwear was not fitted, but, like outer clothes, was wrapped around the body. On this vase a woman wearing a strip of material as a bra is putting her *chiton* over her head.

Chiton

GREEK FANTASY
Sir Lawrence Alma-Tadema (pp. 30–31) often chose classical subjects for his paintings. The architecture and clothing, however, frequently owed more to his imagination than to historical accuracy.

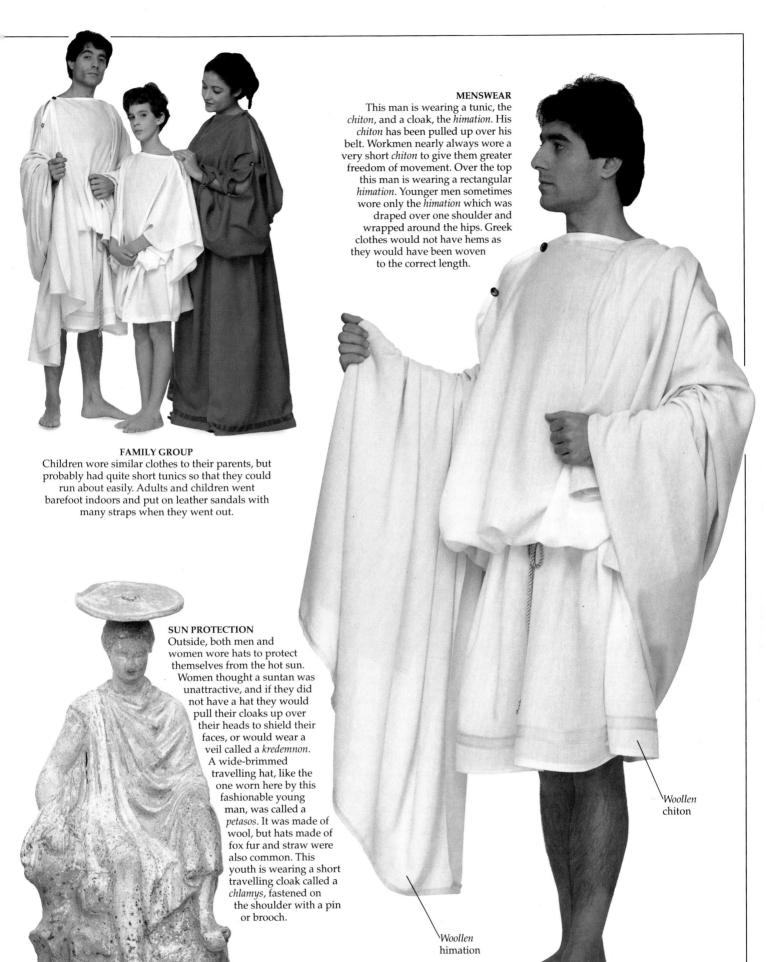

MENSWEAR
This man is wearing a tunic, the *chiton*, and a cloak, the *himation*. His *chiton* has been pulled up over his belt. Workmen nearly always wore a very short *chiton* to give them greater freedom of movement. Over the top this man is wearing a rectangular *himation*. Younger men sometimes wore only the *himation* which was draped over one shoulder and wrapped around the hips. Greek clothes would not have hems as they would have been woven to the correct length.

FAMILY GROUP
Children wore similar clothes to their parents, but probably had quite short tunics so that they could run about easily. Adults and children went barefoot indoors and put on leather sandals with many straps when they went out.

SUN PROTECTION
Outside, both men and women wore hats to protect themselves from the hot sun. Women thought a suntan was unattractive, and if they did not have a hat they would pull their cloaks up over their heads to shield their faces, or would wear a veil called a *kredemnon*. A wide-brimmed travelling hat, like the one worn here by this fashionable young man, was called a *petasos*. It was made of wool, but hats made of fox fur and straw were also common. This youth is wearing a short travelling cloak called a *chlamys*, fastened on the shoulder with a pin or brooch.

Woollen chiton

Woollen himation

The Greek games

CHAMPIONS
This fourth-century B.C. bronze statue of a boy jockey and his victorious horse, show the difficulties of racing in ancient Greece. Riding bare-back and without stirrups, jockeys were usually paid servants of the owners of the horse.

Tʜᴇ GREEKS BELIEVED IN THE VALUE of sport as training for warfare, and as a way of honouring the gods. There were many local sporting competitions, but four big athletic festivals attracted men from all over the Greek world. Of these, the most important was the Olympic Games, held every four years in honour of Zeus at Olympia. Success in the Games brought honour to the athlete's family and to his home town. Some successful athletes acquired almost mythical status. Wars were suspended to allow people to travel in safety to and from Olympia. Many beautiful temples and other buildings which provided facilities for athletes and spectators have been excavated there. The Games went on into Roman times, coming to an end late in the fourth century. In Athens, there were also four-yearly games (Panathenaic Games) held in honour of Athena as part of her religious festival, and they were an important public holiday. Discipline in sport was strict, and breaking the rules was punished severely.

TRAINING TIME
Wrestling, although popular, was regarded as one of the most dangerous of Greek sports. Tripping your opponent up was permitted but biting or gouging out his eyes was strictly forbidden. The man on the left of this statue base is in a racing start position, and the man on the right is testing his javelin.

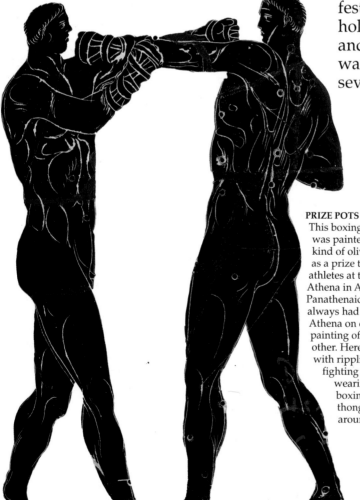

PRIZE POTS
This boxing scene (336 B.C.) was painted on a special kind of olive oil pot given as a prize to victorious athletes at the festival of Athena in Athens. Known as Panathenaic vases, they always had a painting of Athena on one side and a painting of the event on the other. Here, two boxers with rippling muscles are fighting each other wearing, instead of boxing gloves, leather thongs wrapped around their fists.

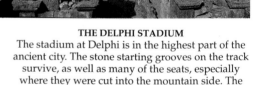

THE DELPHI STADIUM
The stadium at Delphi is in the highest part of the ancient city. The stone starting grooves on the track survive, as well as many of the seats, especially where they were cut into the mountain side. The stadium could hold 7,000 spectators.

THE OLYMPIC SPIRIT
The spirit of the Olympic Games has greatly inspired artists. This 19th-century German duotone depicts naked athletes exercising against a background of classical columns.

THE PENTATHLON
This scene shows athletes taking part in the pentathlon, an event which included discus and javelin throwing, jumping, wrestling, and running. The man at the back holds a pair of jumping weights like the ones shown below.

DEDICATED DISCUS
This bronze discus was made in the sixth century B.C. The inscription on it says that it was thrown by an athlete called Exoidas who won a contest with it, then dedicated the discus to Castor and Pollux, the twin sons of Zeus. Pollux was a champion discus thrower.

THE DISCUS THROWER
This famous marble statue of a discus thrower is a copy of a Greek bronze original, perhaps made by the renowned sculptor, Myron.

TORCHLIGHT
An Olympic runner carrying the Olympic flame at the Seoul Olympics of 1988. In the Athenian games, relay races with torches took place after dark, the winning team lighting a fire on altars to Zeus or Athena.

LONGER JUMPS
Athletes taking part in the long jump, used stone or lead jumping weights. This Roman example had grooves so that it could be gripped firmly. Holding the weights, athletes probably threw their arms backwards to give themselves extra propulsion on take-off.

MODERN GAMES
The Olympic tradition continues today, held every four years and divided between winter and summer Games. Cities all over the world compete intensely to host the Games, building new Olympic stadia and facilities to accommodate the influx of competitors, media, tourism, trade, and foreign currency that goes with setting up the ultimate global sporting event.

THE FIRST MODERN OLYMPICS
The first modern Olympics were held in 1896 in Athens. They were organized by Baron Pierre de Coubertin, a Frenchman, who was inspired by the ideals of the ancient Olympic Games.

Wisdom and beauty

FOR THE GREEKS, PHILOSOPHY, or the "love of wisdom", was something which involved not just the way people lived, but a great deal of science as well. Early thinkers were concerned with ideas about the physical world. Heraclitus developed a theory involving atoms, and Pythagoras came up with his theorem, as part of his view that the world was based on mathematical patterns. He and his fellow thinkers, both men and women, also believed that souls could be reborn in other bodies (reincarnation), and some even thought that beans might contain the souls of old friends and therefore shouldn't be eaten. Philosophy and the arts were part of religion too. Religious hymns celebrated the meaning and mystery of life and explained the origin of the gods. The Greeks made handsome objects both as offerings to the gods and also for their own sakes. Music, sculpture, painting, pottery, and dance all thrived in ancient Greece.

ROYAL PUPIL
Greek philosophers were at the centre of Greek life. Here, the philosopher Aristotle is tutoring the young prince, Alexander of Macedon (pp. 62–63).

PIPED MUSIC
This pipe from Athens made out of sycamore wood, is one of a pair; Greeks played sets of double pipes. There was originally a reed in the mouthpiece, so the pipes would have sounded a bit like a modern oboe.

VASE PAINTER
Vase painting is considered to be one of the minor arts, but the work of the potter and painter Exekias was of a very high standard. This exquisitely painted drinking cup shows the god Dionysos reclining in a boat, with his special plant, the vine, twining around the mast. The god, like the vine, was believed to have come from the east. The dolphins may be the pirates who tried to capture him, now turned into sea creatures.

Pythagoras holding the cosmos

ANIMAL AMPLIFIER
The European tortoise was once plentiful in Greece, and its empty shell made an excellent sound-box for the stringed instrument called the lyre. Its strings, which were plucked with a plectrum, could be tightened to produce a range of notes.

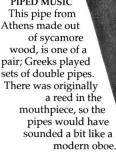

THE KEY TO THE COSMOS
Pythagoras (c.580–500 B.C.) originally from the island of Samos, was the leading light of a group of religious thinkers in southern Italy. They believed that the key to the world (cosmos) lay in numbers and mathematical relationships.

SEEING EYE TO EYE
The eye was an important symbol in ancient Greece. It gave life and power to objects. Statues had their eyes painted in; eyes on the front of warships magically guided them. This eye cup of the sixth century B.C. blends the elements of a face with the patterns found on many wine-cups. The eyebrows are echoed by long strands of ivy, a plant associated with Dionysos. There are a pair of his satyr friends escaping around the sides of the cup. The eyes themselves have perfectly formed circles incised with the sharp point of a pair of dividers.

Cup has no flat base and was probably handed around from hand to hand

DEATH BY HEMLOCK
Socrates' teachings were so astonishing, even for the fairly broad-minded Athenians, that some people became suspicious of him. He was accused of corrupting the minds of the young, and of showing disrespect for the gods. He was imprisoned, then made to take his own life by drinking a poison, hemlock.

WORD OF MOUTH
Although Socrates (469–399 B.C.) is one of the most famous of the ancient Greek philosophers, he produced no philosophical writings. He explored philosophy by intensive discussions, often pretending to be ignorant of a subject, in order to allow his opponents unintentionally to demolish their own case. Socrates has a bare chest in this marble statuette; philosophers were often shown dressed in this way.

FOUNDING FATHERS
Side by side, with proud gestures, philosophers Aristotle (384–322 B.C.) and Plato (427–347 B.C.) are outlined against the sky, each holding one of their major books in their hands. The Italian artist Raphael (1483–1520), has placed them in the very centre of his fresco, painted on the wall of a great room in the Vatican in the early 16th century.

PLATO AND PUPILS
The leading philosophers attracted groups of pupils, and much teaching was done in discussion groups. Plato set up a school for philosophers in Athens, his native city, in a pleasant garden called the Academy. Plato wrote up many ideas of Socrates in the form of "dialogues" or discussions between pupils and teachers.

Vases and vessels

THE BEST GREEK POTTERY was made in Athens. A high-quality clay was found there which fired well to a beautiful reddish-brown colour. Athenian potters worked in a potters' quarter called the *Kerameikos*. They produced huge quantities of wheel-made pottery for use at home and for the export market. There are various styles of decoration in vase painting. Between 1000 and 700 B.C. geometric patterns were the fashion. Gradually, around 720 B.C., oriental motifs came into fashion. The black-figure technique – black silhouette figures painted in a highly-refined clay solution on the reddish clay background – was the main way of decorating pots from the early to mid sixth century B.C. Inner details were incised with a bone or metal tool. Soon after 500 B.C., the red-figure technique took over. The figures of gods and animals were now left in the reddish-brown clay and instead the background was painted in with a clay solution which, in the firing process, turned black. Many vases have been preserved in excellent condition.

Black-figure vase

DRINKING UP TIME
Special drinking cups in the form of animal heads were very popular. This angry-looking griffin *rhyton* is a good example. The wine would have spilt if the *rhyton* was put down, so perhaps it was passed from person to person until all the wine was gone.

Trefoil top

FIRST SIP
This miniature wine jug is called a *chous*. It shows two schoolboys, one reading from a papyrus scroll and the other holding a lyre. The jug would have been filled with wine and given to a little boy as a special present at the festival of Dionysus, god of wine.

WHAT A BOAR!
Stories of the 12 labours of Herakles often appeared on vases (pp. 22–23). On this black-figure vase, Herakles holds the Erymanthian boar above King Eurystheus who cowers in a jar.

The purplish-red colour is a mixture of the black clay solution and a red iron oxide

COLLECTOR'S ITEM
This early 19th-century cartoon shows Sir William Hamilton (pp. 42–43), caricatured as a water pot (*hydria*). Sir William was a great expert on and collector of Greek art, especially vases.

VASE VAULT
In this engraving, Sir William is supervising the opening of a tomb in Italy. The skeleton is surrounded by vases which were exported from Athens.

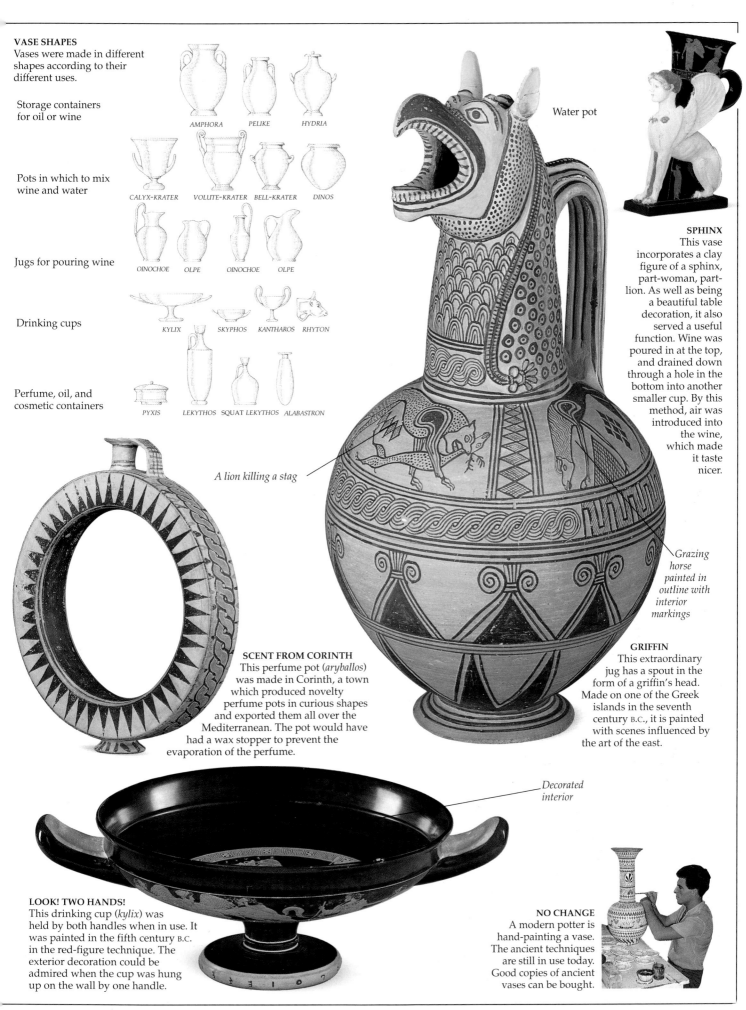

VASE SHAPES
Vases were made in different shapes according to their different uses.

Storage containers for oil or wine

AMPHORA   PELIKE   HYDRIA

Pots in which to mix wine and water

CALYX-KRATER   VOLUTE-KRATER   BELL-KRATER   DINOS

Jugs for pouring wine

OINOCHOE   OLPE   OINOCHOE   OLPE

Drinking cups

KYLIX   SKYPHOS   KANTHAROS   RHYTON

Perfume, oil, and cosmetic containers

PYXIS   LEKYTHOS   SQUAT LEKYTHOS   ALABASTRON

Water pot

A lion killing a stag

Grazing horse painted in outline with interior markings

SPHINX
This vase incorporates a clay figure of a sphinx, part-woman, part-lion. As well as being a beautiful table decoration, it also served a useful function. Wine was poured in at the top, and drained down through a hole in the bottom into another smaller cup. By this method, air was introduced into the wine, which made it taste nicer.

GRIFFIN
This extraordinary jug has a spout in the form of a griffin's head. Made on one of the Greek islands in the seventh century B.C., it is painted with scenes influenced by the art of the east.

SCENT FROM CORINTH
This perfume pot (*aryballos*) was made in Corinth, a town which produced novelty perfume pots in curious shapes and exported them all over the Mediterranean. The pot would have had a wax stopper to prevent the evaporation of the perfume.

Decorated interior

LOOK! TWO HANDS!
This drinking cup (*kylix*) was held by both handles when in use. It was painted in the fifth century B.C. in the red-figure technique. The exterior decoration could be admired when the cup was hung up on the wall by one handle.

NO CHANGE
A modern potter is hand-painting a vase. The ancient techniques are still in use today. Good copies of ancient vases can be bought.

Farming, fishing, and food

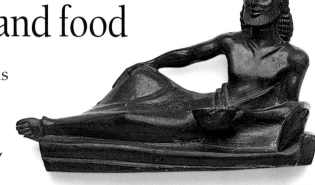

DINNER SERVICE
Wealthy people always took their food and drink while reclining on a couch. Slaves would bring in food and place it on a small table in front of the diner. This bronze banqueter is said to have come from Dodona in north western Greece.

LIFE ON A GREEK FARM was difficult as the soil in much of Greece is of poor quality. Greek farmers ploughed in spring and then again in autumn. Ploughs, which were pulled by oxen, were made of wood and sometimes tipped with iron to make them sharper. The farmworker followed the plough, scattering seed, such as barley, by hand. Farmers prayed to Zeus, and Demeter, goddess of the grain, for a wonderful harvest. On the slopes of the hills there were vineyards and some picked grapes drying in the sun. Other grapes were gathered to make wine, the most popular Greek drink. Most towns and villages were near the sea, and a variety of fish were caught using bronze fish hooks. Wealthy people hunted wild deer, boar, and hare. Poorer people ate meat only on special festival occasions when animals were sacrificed to the gods and then shared out among the worshippers.

TIME STANDS STILL
This shepherd and flock going home for the night look the same as they would have done in ancient times.

HUNTING AND FISHING
This fresco of a Bronze Age fisherman comes from Santorini, a volcanic island near Crete. Perhaps he was bringing the fish as an offering to the palace there. The hunter (a vase painting) is carrying a fox and a hare, while his hunting dog runs beside him. He would not have eaten the fox, but might have made a warm hat from the fur.

The hunter with his dog and prey is taken from a vase

The fisherman with his catch appears on a Cretan fresco

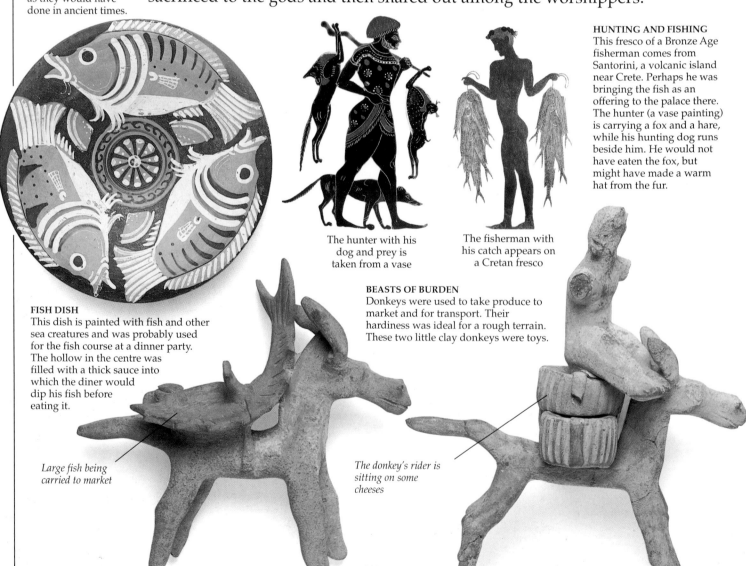

FISH DISH
This dish is painted with fish and other sea creatures and was probably used for the fish course at a dinner party. The hollow in the centre was filled with a thick sauce into which the diner would dip his fish before eating it.

BEASTS OF BURDEN
Donkeys were used to take produce to market and for transport. Their hardiness was ideal for a rough terrain. These two little clay donkeys were toys.

Large fish being carried to market

The donkey's rider is sitting on some cheeses

Duck's head decorates the end of the strainer

SWIMMING IN OIL
This little dolphin skimming over the waves is an oil container, used in food preparation. Dolphins were common around the coasts of Greece.

FINE WINE
Wine was the most popular Greek drink enjoyed at all times of the day. It was quite thick, needed straining, and was nearly always diluted with water. This wine strainer is made of bronze. Many different kinds of utensil and container were used for the storing, serving, and drinking of wine.

ATTIC OIL
Attica, the region around Athens, was famous for its olive groves. Olive oil was used in cooking, washing, and lighting.

OLIVE HARVEST
Olive trees grow abundantly in Greece. On this vase, four people are gathering olives. One is sitting up in the tree, two are shaking the branches with sticks, and, on the ground below, another is gathering the fallen olives in a basket.

Dregs collected in the bottom of the strainer

Fossilized snail on egg

GOAT FOR ALL SEASONS
Goats were very useful animals. They required only rough grazing and their skins provided warm clothing for country people in winter, as well as milk and cheese. This little bronze goat was made about 500 B.C.

EGG CUP
Five hen's eggs in a terracotta cup were found in a tomb on the island of Rhodes. They are over 2,000 years old. Many households kept hens, and eggs were an important part of the daily diet. Funeral offerings of eggs, both real like these or stone or clay imitations, were common in Greek graves. They seem to have been symbols of life after death.

Crafts, travel, and trade

Stone carvers, metal workers, jewellers, shoemakers, and many other craftsmen flourished in the cities of Greece. Their workshops were usually in the centre of town around the *agora*, or market place. People would come to buy their products, and farmers from the countryside would sell their vegetables, fruit, and cheese. There were also weights-and-measures officials, money-changers, acrobats, dancers, and slaves standing on platforms waiting for a buyer. Most ordinary people did not travel far from home (except to war). There were few good roads and the faithful donkey was the most reliable form of transport for shorter journeys. If a Greek wanted to travel a long distance he would usually go by boat around the coast, thereby avoiding the mountains which cover much of the country. There was a great deal of trade between the city-states and the Greek colonies, as well as with other Mediterranean countries. Oil, wine, pottery, and metal work were the main exports.

FISHY BUSINESS
Fishing provides a livelihood for many Greeks today just as it did in ancient times. A modern fisherman on the island of Mykonos is mending his nets.

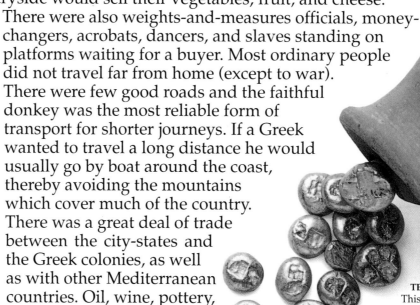

TEMPLE TREASURE
This clay jug with coins was found in the foundations of the temple of Artemis at Ephesus. The coins, made of electrum, probably date from 650–625 B.C. This was soon after coinage was introduced into Greece from Lydia in Asia Minor (roughly, modern Turkey) where coins were invented.

Coin showing the infant Herakles strangling snakes

THREE COINS
Each city-state, as a symbol of independence, issued its own coins which were at first made of electrum (an alloy of gold and silver), and later solely of silver, or occasionally gold. They were often of great beauty, decorated with the symbols of Greek deities and many modern coins have been modelled on them.

Coin showing Cyrus, the king of Persia

A tortoise coin from the island of Aegina

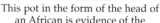

INTO AFRICA
This pot in the form of the head of an African is evidence of the widespread trading contacts of the Greeks. Like most ancient sailors, they preferred to keep the coast within sight where possible.

BEASTS OF BURDEN
Donkeys could negotiate narrow mountain tracks and could carry heavy burdens. They still do today.

COBBLER
This cobbler is depicted at the bottom of a red-figure cup. He is bending over strips of leather which he is cutting and shaping. Boots, sandals, and tools hang from the wall above him. This scene would have become visible to the drinker when he had drained his cup.

AT THE LOOM
Upright looms, just like this one in use today, were used by women in classical times to make woollen clothing, drapes, and furnishing fabrics. Weaving was regarded as a noble, as well as a necessary task.

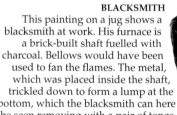

BLACKSMITH
This painting on a jug shows a blacksmith at work. His furnace is a brick-built shaft fuelled with charcoal. Bellows would have been used to fan the flames. The metal, which was placed inside the shaft, trickled down to form a lump at the bottom, which the blacksmith can here be seen removing with a pair of tongs.

POTTER
The Greeks are famous for their beautiful pottery. Every town had its potters' quarter (pp. 48–49) where pots were made and sold. On this wine cup, a potter sits at his wheel, the speed of which he controls with his knee. Above him on a shelf are some of his pots, and below him (now slightly damaged) sits a pet dog who is watching his master at work.

DEEP SEA FISHING
A great variety of fish were available in the deeper waters. Wooden vessels, like this modern one, were used for such fishing expeditions. Eels and salted fish were favourite Greek delicacies.

Warfare

SHIELDED
This Greek vase painting shows how the soldier wears his shield, passing his arm under an iron bar and gripping a leather strap at the rim.

Warfare was a normal part of Greek life, and the city-states frequently fought each other. Many Greek men, therefore, had to join an army, and from the earliest times had to pay for their own armour and equipment. In Athens, boys trained as soldiers between the ages of 18 and 20 after which they could be called up for military service. In Sparta, it was much earlier (pp. 56–57). Athenian soldiers were led by ten commanders called *strategoi*. The infantry soldiers were the backbone of the Greek armies and they fought in close formations called phalanxes. Poorer soldiers served in auxiliary units as archers and stone-slingers. When laying siege to cities, the armies of Hellenistic Greece used catapults, flame-throwers, battering-rams, and cauldrons containing burning coals and sulphur. Athens controlled its empire by means of oar-powered warships or triremes. At the height of its power, Athens could rely on about 300 triremes.

Helmet with nose protection

Body armour

BATTLE OF SALAMIS
The famous sea battle of Salamis was a turning point in the Persian Wars (pp. 18–19). It took place just off the coast of Athens in 480 B.C. and was a triumphant victory for the Greeks over the Persian fleet. As a result of this battle, the Persian king Xerxes and much of his army went back to Asia, abandoning the invasion of Greece.

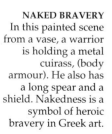

SPEEDY BEASTS
Greek chariots were often decorated with animals associated with speed. These bronze horses were once fixed on to a fast chariot.

NAKED BRAVERY
In this painted scene from a vase, a warrior is holding a metal cuirass, (body armour). He also has a long spear and a shield. Nakedness is a symbol of heroic bravery in Greek art.

HOPLITE
Greek soldiers were called hoplites from the word *hoplon* meaning shield. Only men from wealthy families could be hoplites, because only they could afford expensive armour and weapons.

Greaves

FOOT COMBAT
A painted vase shows two Greek combatants separated by a herald.

HELMETS
Helmets protected the head from every sort of slash and from blows and knocks. They varied in shape and some had crests made of horse hair to make the wearer appear more impressive and frightening.

Attic helmet has no nose guard

Corinthian helmet with long nose-piece and cheek guards

BREASTPLATE
The breastplate, or cuirass, was usually, although not always, made of bronze. It was the main piece of body armour protecting all the upper organs. Cuirasses were made to measure, each man being specially fitted. The more expensive cuirasses would have ridges, roughly aligned to the body muscles, which were meant to deflect blows. The cuirass was made of two plates joined at the sides by leather straps. The side areas, therefore, were the most vulnerable parts of the body.

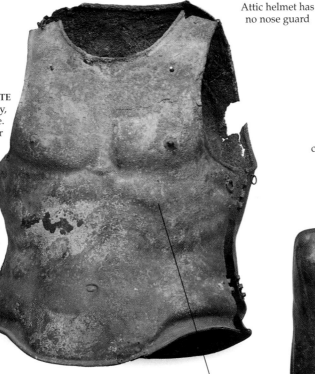

Sculpted ridges roughly aligning with chest muscles

GREAVES
Hoplites wore bronze leg guards called greaves (below) to protect the lower part of their legs in battle. Some of these greaves may have originally been fixed on to large statues of heroic warriors in southern Italy.

WARSHIP
The fastest Greek ship was called a trireme and it needed 170 oarsmen to row it. They sat in three levels, one above the other, on either side of the boat. At the prow was a pointed ram strengthened with metal, which could sink enemy ships. There was often an eye painted on the prow (pp. 46–47). This illustration shows two sails, but warships may have had only one, probably made of linen and lowered when the ship was engaged in battle.

The long spear was the main weapon of the Greek infantry

CHAMPION FIGHT
This red-figure vase shows a fight between two heroes of the Trojan War, Achilles and Hektor (pp. 12–13). The vase painter has clearly painted the blood flowing from the wound just above Hektor's knee. Both heroes are wearing the crested helmets and armour worn by infantry soldiers of the 5th century B.C.

The state of Sparta

HARBOUR BATTLE
The Piraeus is the port of Athens, 6 km (4 miles) to the southwest of the city. In this engraving it is being besieged by Spartan ships in 388 B.C.

SPARTA IN SOUTHERN GREECE WAS FOUNDED in the tenth century B.C. by the Dorians, who defeated the original inhabitants of the area. Two centuries later, Sparta conquered its neighbour, Messenia, and gained excellent agricultural land. It became a luxury-loving state producing fine crafts. Music and poetry also flourished. Later, the Spartans were defeated in war, and the conquered Messenians engaged in a long-running rebellion, so Sparta turned to military matters. It became a super-power in Greece and the main rival of Athens, and Spartan society was dominated by the need to maintain power. All men of Spartan birth had to serve in the army. Their whole lives were dedicated to learning the arts of war. Boys of seven were taken from their families to live in army barracks. Non-citizens in Sparta were either *perioikoi* or *helots*. The *perioikoi* were free men who, although they did not have the rights of citizens, were allowed to trade, and serve in the army. *Helots* were the descendants of the original inhabitants of the area. They farmed the land and did all the heavy work for their Spartan overlords.

NATURAL PROTECTION
This 19th-century German engraving shows the site of Sparta in a fertile plain of Lakonia in southern Greece. Its remoteness was an advantage to the warring Spartans and the high mountains to the east, north, and west, and the sea to the south, formed natural defences.

SPARTAN WARRIOR
The Greek historian Herodotus wrote that Spartan soldiers, like this one of the fifth century B.C., always combed their long hair when they felt they might be about to put their lives at risk, as when going into battle. The scarlet colour of the military cloaks became a symbol of Spartan pride.

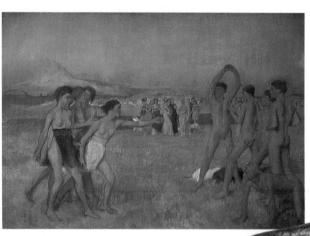

THE YOUNG SPARTANS
Spartan scenes were a popular subject with artists of the 19th century. This unusual painting by French impressionist painter Edgar Degas (1834–1917) shows boys and girls exercising in the valley of the river Eurotas which runs through Sparta. The girls look much more aggressive than girls from other Greek cities.

SPARTAN REGIME
The Spartan system of education, with its emphasis on physical fitness, was much admired in 19th-century Victorian Britain. Corporal punishment too was regarded as character-forming for schoolboys, just as it was in ancient Sparta. The violence of this cartoon by British cartoonist George Cruikshank (1792–1878) suggests that he thought otherwise.

56

OFFERINGS
Hundreds of thousands of small figurines have been found at a sanctuary of Artemis Orthia on the banks of the river Eurotas at Sparta. Among animals such as stags, dogs, and horses are representations of Artemis herself. There are also figurines of the goddess Athena wearing a helmet. The figurines were made at the sanctuary and sold to visitors who often left them behind as offerings to the goddess. It was to this sanctuary that Spartan boys were taken to be flogged as a demonstration of their toughness and endurance.

Artemis

Warrior

Artemis

Figure playing pipes

A stag

IN THE LEAD
This girl is taking part in a running race and is looking back to see how far she is in the lead. She is wearing a very short skirt which no girl from any other Greek city would dare to wear. Girls did not fight in wars but, like most boys, they were trained in running and for an outdoor life. This made them fit and strong so that they would have healthy babies who would grow up to be good soldiers.

Science and medicine

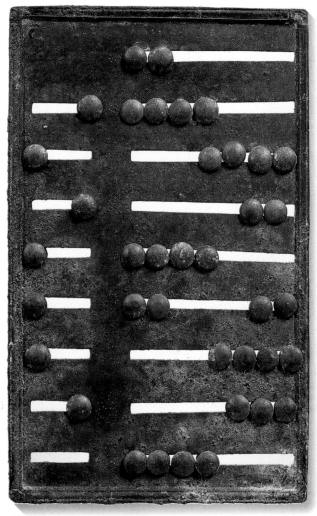

ASCLEPIADES
Asclepiades was a famous Greek doctor of the first century B.C. He was very knowledgeable in the theory and practice of medicine, but he also believed in wine as an aid to recovery and the importance of a pleasant bedside manner, so he was very popular with all his patients.

THE GREEKS WERE INTERESTED in science and, influenced by Egyptian and Babylonian scholars, made advances in biology, mathematics, astronomy, and geography. In the third century B.C., the astronomer, Aristarchus, already understood that the earth revolved around the sun, and another astronomer, Anaxagoras (500–428 B.C.), discovered that the moon reflected sunlight. The most advanced scientific work took place in Hellenistic times (pp. 62–63). An important area of Greek science was medicine. The Greeks believed that illness was a punishment sent by the gods to whom they prayed for a cure. Sanctuaries of the god Asclepius (the god of medicine) were found all over the Greek world. The most famous one was at Epidaurus. Many sick people came there and spent the night in the temple. They believed that Asclepius appeared to them in "dreams" to prescribe treatments such as herbal remedies, diets, and exercises. The next day, the priests would carry out the treatment and many people went away cured. The Greeks developed sophisticated medical treatments for all kinds of diseases. These treatments, based on practical research, grew out of the Asclepiad cult and were practised by Hippocrates (460–377 B.C.) who is often described as the founder of modern medicine.

ABACUS
The Greeks used a counting frame called an abacus for mathematical calculations. It had beads threaded in lines on wires. Some lines had beads which counted as 1, others had the value of 10 and others, 100. By moving the beads around, complicated multiplication and division could be achieved.

IT ALL ADDS UP
This engraving from the *Margarita Philosophica* of 1496 shows the Roman philosopher Boethius (A.D. 480–524) doing mathematical calculations, and the Greek mathematician Pythagoras (pp. 46–47) working at an abacus. The woman in the centre is probably a muse of learning.

TEMPLE OF ASCLEPIUS
In this engraving, people can be seen approaching a statue of the god Asclepius. He is sitting on a throne and holding his staff which has a serpent twisted round it. A real snake, regarded as sacred and kept in all temples to Asclepius, can be seen slithering along the plinth.

TEMPLE VISIT
In this painting by the 19th-century artist John William Waterhouse (1849–1917) a child has been brought by his mother to the temple of Asclepius. Priests of the god stand around waiting to interpret his wishes.

THANKS

Patients who had been cured by Asclepius often left a model of the part of their body affected by illness, as an offering of thanks to the god for curing them. This marble relief of a leg has an inscription to Asclepius carved upon it and was dedicated by a worshipper called Tyche.

HIPPOCRATES

The famous physician, Hippocrates, was born on the island of Kos. He wrote 53 scientific books on medical topics, now known as the *Corpus*. He taught that the human body was a single organism and each part could only be understood in the context of the whole. Modern doctors still take the Hippocratic Oath which is the basis of medical ethics.

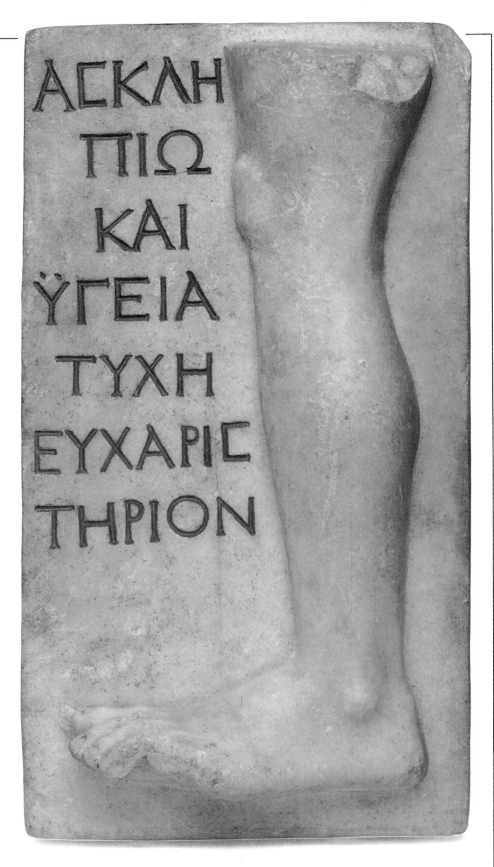

ΑΣΚΛΗ
ΠΙΩ
ΚΑΙ
ΫΓΕΙΑ
ΤΥΧΗ
ΕΥΧΑΡΙϹ
ΤΗΡΙΟΝ

MODERN MODELS

The practice of leaving a model of the affected part of the body as a thanks offering, still continues in churches in some countries today. These modern examples are from Athens.

TOKENS

These modern silver tokens are also thanks for cures. The animals indicate that people believed that they too could be cured with the help of offerings.

Death and the afterlife

D<small>EATH CAME EARLY</small> for most people in ancient times, because life was very harsh. Young men often died in battle and young women in childbirth. The Greeks believed in – or hoped for – some kind of life after death, although their ideas about this state varied. The kingdom of the dead was generally thought to be deep in the earth, and therefore many people buried their dead. But sometimes corpses were cremated on a funeral pyre. The soul was sometimes shown as a tiny winged person, and some Greeks believed that it escaped from the body and rose up to become one of the stars, waiting until it could be reborn in a new body. Gods, such as Dionysus, who, like the vines he protected, died and was reborn each year, gave people hope of new life. The goddess of the grain, Demeter, whose daughter Persephone was snatched away by Hades, the god of the underworld, claimed back her daughter for part of the year (spring and summer) too. Tombs were decorated with pictures of feasts and the dead person's favourite things, and food was placed in the grave, so that the dead could be happy in the afterlife.

KING OF THE UNDERWORLD
Zeus ruled the earth and sky, Poseidon, the sea. The third of these divine brothers was Hades, king of the underworld, also known as Pluto. Eventually the underworld came to be known simply as Hades.

THE DIVER
This delightful painting was found on the inside of a stone sarcophagus (coffin) found at Poseidonia, a Greek city in southern Italy, later called Paestum. It probably represents the leap of the dead into the unknown.

FLASK OF FAREWELL
Offerings to the dead included narrow flasks known as *lekythoi*, which contained oil used to anoint the body. They were decorated with delicately painted scenes of farewell. This dead warrior, perhaps a victim of one of the many wars in fifth-century Greece, receives his helmet from a woman. The goose at their feet, the bird of Aphrodite (pp. 20–21) hints at their relationship.

FARE FOR THE FERRYMAN

Charon was the grim ferryman who carried people across the black waters of the river Styx and into the kingdom of the dead. In this painting by John Stanhope (pp. 12–13), the underworld is a gloomy place with whispering reeds and spindly trees through which dead souls can be seen making their way to the river. The one way trip in Charon's punt cost one obol. The family of the dead sometimes left a coin on the corpse for the journey.

THE ENTRANCE TO HADES

Ancient people thought that certain places might be the entrance to the underworld. Many Greeks had settled near Solfatara in southern Italy, where the steaming sulphur lake made it a prime candidate.

DEATH BEFORE DISHONOUR

After the death of Achilles, the great warrior Ajax failed to become the champion of the Greeks fighting at Troy. He could not live with the shame, so killed himself by falling on his sword. This famous incident from the Trojan War is often shown on painted pots and is also the subject of a great play by Sophokles (pp. 38–39).

TOMBSTONE

In Athens at certain periods, tombstones, carved in marble and originally painted in bright colours, were placed above graves. Above the carving of the dead person, the sloping lines of a roof suggested a temple or shrine. Here the dead man, Xanthippos, sits on an elegant curved chair, his children shown on a smaller scale beside him. His name is carved above him. It is not really known why he was holding a foot, but possibly he was a shoemaker.

MOURNING LINE

A Greek funeral was a dramatic event. The body was laid out on a couch, with the feet facing the door to ensure that the spirit would leave. A wreath was placed on the head. A procession of mourners wearing black robes escorted the corpse. The women cut off their long hair as a sign of grief and gave a lock of it to the dead person. They also tore at their cheeks until the blood ran.

Alexander and the Hellenistic age

EXCAVATION AT EPHESUS
Ephesus was a teeming city on the coast of Asia Minor where Greeks and people of many other nationalities lived together. The city and its famous sanctuary, dedicated to the goddess Artemis, thrived in the Hellenistic period and throughout the Roman period.

IN THE FOURTH CENTURY B.C., a strong king called Philip II turned Macedonia, in the north, into the most powerful state in Greece. After his assassination in 337 B.C., his 20-year-old son Alexander, a military genius, took over the reins of power. Not content with ruling Greece, he invaded Persian territory in 334 B.C., and then pressed on through Asia Minor, then south and east to Egypt, Afghanistan, and India. He established new Greek cities, such as Alexandria in Egypt, and thus spread Greek culture over a vast area. Alexander, called the Great, intended to create a huge empire, incorporating most of the then known world. His death of a fever in 323 B.C. ended this ambition, and instead, his vast empire was divided up among his quarrelling generals. The period from the death of Alexander until about 30 B.C. is known as the Hellenistic Age from the word "Hellene" meaning Greek. The Hellenistic kingdoms preserved many aspects of Greek life but they were eventually overcome by the rising power of Rome.

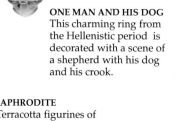

ONE MAN AND HIS DOG
This charming ring from the Hellenistic period is decorated with a scene of a shepherd with his dog and his crook.

APHRODITE
Terracotta figurines of Aphrodite, goddess of love and beauty, were popular in Hellenistic times. She is nearly always shown without any clothes, sometimes tying a ribbon in her hair, sometimes bending down to fasten her sandal.

Ruins at Pergamum

TOWN PLANNING
Pergamum, a Hellenistic city in Asia Minor, was the power base of the wealthy Attalid dynasty. The ruins of temples and other opulent civic buildings can still be seen on the terraces cut into the steep mountain site. The people of Pergamum must have enjoyed spectacular views over the surrounding countryside.

Ruins at Pergamum

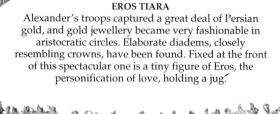

EROS TIARA
Alexander's troops captured a great deal of Persian gold, and gold jewellery became very fashionable in aristocratic circles. Elaborate diadems, closely resembling crowns, have been found. Fixed at the front of this spectacular one is a tiny figure of Eros, the personification of love, holding a jug.

ALEXANDER'S EMPIRE

Alexander did not just want to build an empire, he also wanted it to last. To stop rebellion and invasion by conquered peoples, he founded many colonies populated by his own former soldiers who followed the Greek way of life. On the whole he treated the conquered peoples with respect and encouraged his men to marry eastern women. His conquests came to an end in India because his men refused to fight any further.

Richard Burton in the 1956 film *Alexander the Great*

TRUNK CHARGER
This coin shows Alexander on horseback attacking two Indian warriors mounted on an elephant. It is thought to have been issued in Babylon in 323 B.C.

WALL OF FIRE
In 327 B.C., Alexander crossed the Himalayan mountains intending to conquer India. But a terrible battle forced him to return to Babylon. Alexander's fame lived on in legend. This Indian painting, painted over 1,000 years after his time, shows him building a defensive wall of fire.

THE DEFEAT OF DARIUS
Alexander finally defeated the Persian king Darius III in a long and bloody battle at Gaugamela in Mesopotamia (south-west Asia) in 331 B.C., and Darius fled. After this, Alexander called himself "King of Asia". In this etching, he can be seen on horseback, fighting fearlessly.

FAMILY OF DARIUS
In this painting by the Italian artist Paolo Veronese (1528–1588), Alexander is shown receiving the submission of the family of his defeated enemy Darius. Notice that the artist has dressed everyone in 16th-century clothes.

Did you know?

Lion Gate, Mycenae, erected in the thirteenth century B.C.

The prehistoric Mycenaeans built such huge stone walls around their citadels – some of them were 14 m (46 ft) wide – that later civilizations believed they were the work of giants.

The distinctive proportions and one-foot-forward stance typical of kouroi (male nude temple statues) were adopted from ancient Egyptian figures. Monumental in size, they were idealized rather than naturalistic in style.

Slaves were very important to the economy of ancient Greece. Some had very hard lives, but many were respectfully treated and well educated. Those taken prisoner by the Romans after their conquest were highly prized, and some worked as teachers and doctors.

Greek theatres, with their tiered seating, were very sophisticated in terms of sight lines and sound amplification. They had to be built into natural slopes, though, since the Greeks did not have the engineering skills to support the necessary height and weight of the buildings on flat ground.

Archimedes, legendary mathematician and scientist, was murdered by the Romans in 212 B.C. during their conquest of Greek territories. This conquest was complete by 146 B.C.

Pan, Greek god of fields, shepherds and woodlands, was believed to have a terrifying voice, which could paralyse animals with fear, stop armies from advancing and topple city walls. The god's name is the root of our word *panic*.

The apparently upright, tapering columns on the Parthenon actually lean inwards slightly and bulge in the middle. This is to compensate for the effects of perspective, which visually distorts straight lines and accurate alignments. For the same reason, the Parthenon frieze is sculpted in deeper relief towards the top, and the building's base and steps are imperceptibly higher in the middle than at the edges.

No mortar was used in the construction of Greek temples: stone blocks were smoothly fitted together and held with metal clamps and dowels.

The ancient Greeks established a tradition of making and decorating pottery that lasted for over 1,000 years. Certainly, some of the objects they produced would look very strange to us – cups and bottles, for example, that could not be set down on a flat surface because they had curved or pointed bases. Many others, though, such as simple rounded jugs and storage pots, are almost exactly the same as the ones in a twenty-first century kitchen.

Colour was very important to the ancient Greeks, especially in the Hellenistic period (from 323 to about 30 B.C.). In fact, many of the white marble statues we associate with this time were once brightly painted.

Alexander the Great was given his horse Bucephalus, when he was 12 years old. No adult could control the animal, but Alexander discovered that the horse was frightened of his own shadow, so he calmed him by turning his head to the sun.

Greek god Pan playing a lyre

Macedonian soldiers originated a battle line called a phalanx, in which they would huddle close together forming a compact mass with their shields. This powerful unit would then push and shove its way through enemy lines.

The Greeks invented picture mosaics in the fifth century B.C. They used the new technique to decorate their floors with elaborate mythological scenes. The first mosaics were made from coloured pebbles, but these were later replaced with specially cut cubes of glass, stone or marble called *tesserae*, which produced finer detail and a larger range of colours.

Alexander and his horse

QUESTIONS AND ANSWERS

Q What happened when the ancient Greeks consulted the Oracle of Apollo at Delphi?

A Those who wanted advice from the Oracle would be required to pay a levy and sacrifice an animal on the altar. A male priest would then put the petitioner's question to a priestess, whose trance-like reply would take the form of riddles. These riddles would then be interpreted by a priest in a manner that was still not straightforward, but open to a number of interpretations.

Q Why was Delphi considered a sacred place?

A According to legend, the god Zeus released two eagles from opposite ends of the Earth. Their paths crossed above Delphi, which established it as the centre of the world, and a sacred site. The spot was originally marked out with a navel stone or omphalos, a Hellenistic copy of which can be seen in the Delphi Museum. The young god Apollo was thought to live at Delphi, which is why, from the end of the eighth century B.C., people came here to ask his advice.

Temple of Apollo at Delphi

Q Where did traditional Greek drama come from?

A Greek drama developed in the sixth century B.C. from ritual role-playing during festivals of Dionysus, the god of revelry and wine. At first, the participants danced in groups and were often dressed as animals. Later, singing and dancing choruses were joined by actors wearing masks with exaggerated features to indicate the characters they were playing so they could be clearly seen by everyone in the audience. The first proper plays were tragedies in the form of episodes from myths and epic poems. They were staged in sets of three, all written by the same person. Comedy did not appear on the Greek stage until about 480 B.C.

Q Where did the tradition of the marathon run come from?

A In 490 B.C., the Greeks were facing invasion by Darius of Persia, whose warships landed in the Bay of Marathon. Despite being heavily outnumbered, the Greeks surrounded the enemy troops and drove them back to the sea, losing only 192 men during the fighting, while 6,000 Persians perished. News of the victory was taken back to Athens – a distance of 41 km (26 miles) – by a runner in full armour, who collapsed and died immediately afterwards. The modern marathon has its roots in this heroic effort.

Q Why is classical Greek architecture so widely admired?

A State and religious buildings in ancient Greece were designed and built with the express intention of embodying perfect form and proportion. The degree of success their architects achieved is illustrated by the fact that their classical style has survived, has seldom fallen out of fashion and has often dominated aesthetic taste. Superb examples were built in revolutionary France, Georgian England, the newly formed United States and nineteenth-century Athens, where Neoclassical architecture completely dominated public building (see page 69).

Record Breakers

FIRST OF THE GREATS
The Greek warrior king Alexander (356-323 B.C.) was the first leader to be widely known as "the Great". During his short life, he founded 70 cities, several of which were named Alexandria after him.

EARLY LEARNING
Aristotle, a pupil of Socrates, founded the Lyceum in Athens where subjects as diverse as biology and ethics could be taught. This institution turned Athens into one of the first university cities in the world.

FIRST STONE THEATRE
The first stone theatre ever built, and the birthplace of Greek tragedy, was the Theatre of Dionysus, which was cut into the southern cliff face of the Acropolis. The remains of a restored and redesigned Roman version can still be seen there today.

EARLY RECORDS
The first accurately documented event in Greek history was the establishment of the Olympic Games in 776 B.C. Named for the Sanctuary of Olympia on the Peloponnese peninsula, where they were held, the games originally had only one event – men's sprinting – and the runners were all local. Later, other competitions, such as wrestling, boxing, jumping, javelin throwing and riding, were added, and the games were thrown open to people from other parts of Greece.

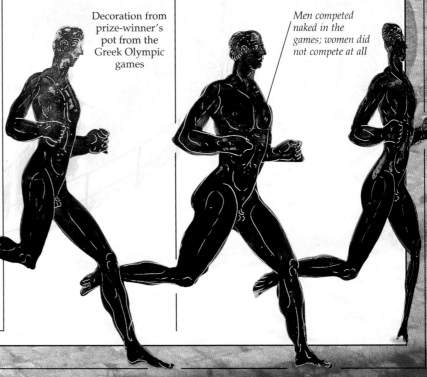

Decoration from prize-winner's pot from the Greek Olympic games

Men competed naked in the games; women did not compete at all

Who's who?

NO OTHER SINGLE CULTURE has influenced western civilization more profoundly than that of ancient Greece. Over a period of a few hundred years, this warm land between the Mediterranean, Aegean and Ionian Seas produced an unequalled collection of statesmen, writers and artists, men of science and great thinkers whose ideas and innovations are still widely valued.

ΠΕΡΙΚΛΗΣ

Statue of Perikles

STATESMEN

SOLON
Athenian legislator and magistrate during the seventh and sixth centuries B.C., whose legal, economic and political reforms represented the birth of democracy.

THEMISTOKLES
Leader of Athens and creator of the powerful fleet that overpowered the Persians at the battle of Salamis in 480 B.C.

PERIKLES
Powerful general and great democratic leader of Athens in the fifth century B.C. Cultured and incorruptible, Perikles masterminded an extensive public building programme that included the Acropolis.

ALEXANDER THE GREAT
Born to Philip II of Macedonia in 356 B.C. and taught by Aristotle, Alexander expanded the Greek Empire into Persia, Asia Minor, Egypt, Afghanistan and India before he died at age 33.

Eighteenth-century relief portrait of Alexander the Great

WRITERS AND ARTISTS

PHEIDIAS
The most famous artist of the ancient world (he died around 432 B.C.), he was celebrated in his own time for two giant statues, one of Athena and one of Zeus. Neither statue still exists, and today he is best known for the Parthenon carvings, which he designed and supervised.

AESCHYLUS
One of three playwrights (with Euripides and Sophokles) dominating Athenian drama in the fifth century B.C. A soldier who fought at Marathon, Aeschylus produced nearly 90 plays, including *Prometheus Bound* and the *Oresteia*.

EURIPIDES
Athenian playwright (see above) who created epic tragedies in the fifth century B.C., with themes of betrayal, murder and injustice. Surviving examples of his plays include *Medea* and *Alcestis*.

SOPHOKLES
Athenian poet and playwright of the fifth century B.C. (see above), known for morality tales such as *Ajax* and *Antigone*.

MYRON
Athenian sculptor of the fifth century B.C. With much of his work lost, Myron is best known today for his bronze statue *The Discus Thrower*, which survives only as Roman copies.

The Discus Thrower (also known as *Discobulus*)

This Roman copy is made of marble

SAPPHO
Lyric poetess who led a group of female writers on the Aegean island of Lesbos in the seventh century B.C. Sappho wrote mainly about family and female friends.

THINKERS

Socrates

PYTHAGORAS
Philosopher and mathematician of the sixth century B.C. who believed that the secrets of life lay in mathematics.

HERODOTUS
Fifth-century B.C. historian, known as the father of history, who produced the first prose accounts of current events, such as the Greek war with the Persians.

THUCYDIDES
Another historian of the fifth century B.C., Thucydides documented the Peloponnesian war between Athens and Sparta using a very analytical approach.

SOCRATES
Renowned fifth-century B.C. thinker who produced no written work, but instead explored ideas through discussion. His talks, as documented by his pupil, Plato, are known as "dialogues".

PLATO
Pupil of Socrates who recorded his teacher's work and set up an Academy in Athens. Plato, too, believed in dialogues, and he produced two well-known treatises, *The Republic* and *The Laws*. Plato was also one of the greatest Greek prose writers.

ARISTOTLE
Fourth-century B.C. pupil of Plato and founder of the Lyceum, Aristotle had an outstanding gift for scientific observation, and one of his most valued legacies is a treatise on Ethics.

EPICURUS
Greek philosopher during the fourth and third centuries B.C. He taught that genuine human happiness is the highest good, and he encouraged its responsible pursuit. Author of a 37-book treatise called *On Nature*, he founded the Epicurean school of philosophy.

SCIENTISTS

Hippocrates

ANAXAGORAS
Astronomer of the fifth century B.C. who discovered that the moon reflects light from the sun.

HIPPOCRATES
Founder of modern medicine in the fifth and fourth centuries B.C., Hippocrates practised it according to the strict ethical standard doctors still adhere to today in the Hippocratic Oath. He also discovered the pain-killing effects of willow bark, from which modern scientists extracted aspirin.

ARISTARCHUS
Third-century B.C. astronomer who understood that the Earth revolves around the Sun and that it rotates on its own axis.

ASCLEPIADES
Physician of the first century B.C. who was learned in medicine and compassionate in his treatment of patients. In common with some modern practitioners, he advocated holistic, non-invasive treatments. His treatments included such things as wine, massage, and bathing.

MODERN CLASSICISTS

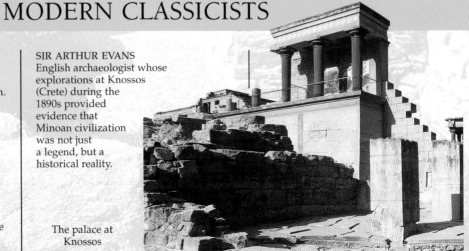

SIR WILLIAM HAMILTON
Early nineteenth-century British diplomat and expert on Greek art. His collection of vases was acquired by the British Museum.

HEINRICH SCHLIEMANN
German amateur archaeologist who, in 1870, discovered the site of ancient Troy near the Turkish coast. This discovery supplied a factual basis for Homer's epic tales of the Trojan war.

PIERRE DE COUBERTIN
Aristocratic Frenchman who, inspired by the original Olympic games, organized the first modern revival in Athens in 1896.

SIR ARTHUR EVANS
English archaeologist whose explorations at Knossos (Crete) during the 1890s provided evidence that Minoan civilization was not just a legend, but a historical reality.

The palace at Knossos

Find out more

THE INFLUENCE OF ANCIENT GREECE has spread throughout almost every country in the western world, and most major museums have a section devoted to Greek art and antiquities. Perhaps the culture's best-known and most powerful symbol, however, is the fortified citadel complex of the Acropolis in Athens with its sacred centre, the Parthenon.

Created as a temple to Athena, patron goddess of Athens, the Parthenon was completely symmetrical. It was constructed of stone and locally quarried white marble, an ideal medium for the detailed relief panels on the frieze and portico. During its long history, the Parthenon has been a church, a mosque and even an arsenal, but today, its inspiring ruins are a popular tourist attraction and a place of pilgrimage for anyone with a fascination for the classical world.

THE PARTHENON
Completed in the mid-fifth century B.C., the Parthenon was designed by the architects Kallikrates and Iktinos to house a monumental 12 m (40 ft) statue of Athena sculpted by Pheidias. When the temple was new, the carvings above the outside row of columns were painted in blue, red and gold.

Skillful carving gives an impression of great depth

THE PARTHENON FRIEZE
The carved frieze that ran around the inner wall of the Parthenon was designed by Pheidias, the artist responsible for all the carving and sculpture in the temple. The individual segments of the frieze are called *metopes*; together they portray a procession of worshippers taking part in the Panathenaic festival, which was held every four years to celebrate Athena's birthday. This section is on display at the British Museum.

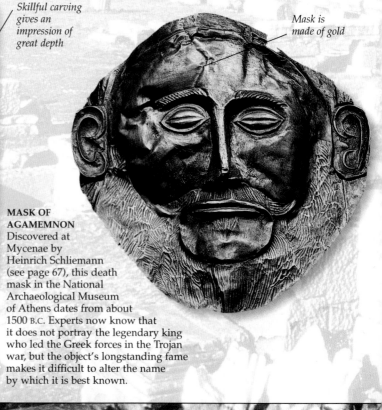

Mask is made of gold

MASK OF AGAMEMNON
Discovered at Mycenae by Heinrich Schliemann (see page 67), this death mask in the National Archaeological Museum of Athens dates from about 1500 B.C. Experts now know that it does not portray the legendary king who led the Greek forces in the Trojan war, but the object's longstanding fame makes it difficult to alter the name by which it is best known.

USEFUL WEBSITES

- Comprehensive general information site:
  www.ancientgreece.com
- Greek Ministry of Culture official website, with listings of archaeological sites, monuments and relevant exhibitions:
  www.culture.gr
- General ancient Greece site with individual links to specific areas of interest:
  www.crystalinks.com/greece.html
- Main British Museum website with a link to ancient Greece
  www.thebritishmuseum.ac.uk/compass
- General information site for designed for children:
  www.historyforkids.org
- Specialist site focussed on ancient Greek dress:
  www.costumes.org/pages/timelinepages/ancientgreece1.htm

Places to visit

THE ACROPOLIS, ATHENS, GREECE
Although access to the temples is restricted to protect them from further damage, the Acropolis still offers a unique collection of ancient sites and exhibits, including:
- the Parthenon
- the Propylaia and the Beule Gate, historical entrances to the complex
- the Theatre of Dionysos, birthplace of Greek tragedy, built in 342-326 B.C.
- the Acropolis Museum, which displays a wealth of treasures from the site, including statues and architectural details such as caryatids, pediments and segments of the Parthenon frieze.

ANCIENT DELPHI, GREECE
First excavated at the end of the nineteenth century, this site encompasses:
- the Sanctuary of Apollo
- the Castalian Spring, where visitors were required to bathe
- the Delphi Museum, whose collection is second in importance only to that of the Acropolis.

NATIONAL ARCHAEOLOGICAL MUSEUM, ATHENS, GREECE
Housed in a nineteenth-century building that has been constantly expanded and improved, this is one of the world's most important collections. Among its treasures are:
- the gold mask of Agamemnon, c1500 B.C., which was found at Mycenae
- superb examples of classical sculpture, including the Marathon Boy dating from c340 B.C.

BRITISH MUSEUM, LONDON, UK
One of the finest collection of Greek antiquities in the world is on display here. Look for:
- the Parthenon marbles (also known as the Elgin marbles) – sculptures and sections of the frieze brought to England by Lord Elgin in the early nineteenth century
- a huge statue from the Mausoleum at Halicarnassus, one of the Seven Wonders of the Ancient World.

METROPOLITAN MUSEUM OF ART, NEW YORK, USA
With a dedicated area that extends over both its main floors, the Metropolitan Museum's Greek and Roman galleries feature:
- a large collection of ancient Greek vases
- important examples of painting and sculpture that illustrate the classical mastery of naturalism in art.

HERMITAGE MUSEUM, MOSCOW, RUSSIAN FEDERATION
Spanning the period from 2000 B.C. to the fourth century A.D., the ancient Greek department of the Hermitage is particularly strong on pottery, including:
- a remarkable display of black-figure vases, including a *hydria* adorned with a scene of Herakles and the Triton
- an equally distinguished collection of red-figure vases by important ceramists of the period.

GREEK THEATRE
This drawing of the character Creon from Sophokcles' play *Antigone* comes from an 1899 issue of the French magazine *La Theatre*. The study of Greek theatrical tradition is one way we have been able to learn about classical Greek culture.

Harvesters hit the branches with sticks to release the olives

PAINTED JAR
Two-handled vessels with narrowed necks are called *amphoras*, and they were designed to store liquid (oil, wine or water) or foods preserved in liquid. The detailed scene of olive-gathering painted on this example from the British Museum suggests that it was intended for olives or olive oil.

NATIONAL ARCHAEOLOGICAL MUSEUM, ATHENS
Opened in 1891, this museum displays an enormous number of Greek works of art that had previously been stored all over the city. Designed in the Neoclassical style that harks back to Greece's golden age, the building's entrance is dominated by Ionic and Corinthian columns.

MARATHON BOY
Found on the sea floor, like many other Greek bronzes, this graceful nude (in the National Archaeological Museum, Athens), is thought to be the work of the sculptor Praxiteles, who was active in the fourth century B.C.

Glossary

ABACUS Ancient counting frame made up of small beads threaded on wires.

ACANTHUS Plant with thick scalloped leaves that often adorn Greek art and architecture. The capital on a Corinthian column is covered with acanthus leaves. (*see also* CAPITAL, CORINTHIAN)

Acanthus capital

AGORA Open market or public space in ancient Greece. Our modern term *agoraphobia*, meaning fear of public places, comes from this word.

AMPHORA Two-handled jar with a narrow neck and sometimes a tapered base, designed for wine, olive oil or other liquid.

ANDRON Small, domestic dining room where men would entertain their friends.

ARYBALLOS Perfume pot, usually made of pottery. These vessels were often in the shape of a fantasy creature or a real animal, such as a monkey or a hedgehog.

Colonnade

ATLANTES Carved male figure used as a column in classical architecture. (*see also* CARYATID, COLUMN)

ASSEMBLY Gathering of people and officials that controlled public life in ancient Athens. There had to be at least 6,000 present to make an Assembly, which decided on important matters of law and state. (*see also* COUNCIL)

CAPITAL The top section of an architectural column. (*see also* COLUMN, CORINTHIAN, DORIC, IONIC, ORDER)

CARYATID Carved female figure used as a supporting column in classical architecture. (*see also* COLUMN, ATLANTES)

CHITON Basic item of clothing for both men and women in ancient Greece. Chitons were made from two rectangles of fabric fastened at the shoulders and down the sides, and tied at the waist. (*see also* PEPLOS)

CITY-STATE A conventional city that, with its surrounding territory, is also an independent political state.

COLUMN A slender, upright structure used in architecture to support an arch, a roof, an upper story or the top part of a wall. Most columns consist of a base, shaft (the main part) and capital (the decorative section at the top). (*see also* ORDER, CAPITAL)

COLONNADE Line of columns supporting a row of arches, a roof, an upper storey or the top part of a wall.

CORINTHIAN One of three principal styles (or orders) in classical architecture. Corinthian columns fall between those of the Doric and Ionic orders in diameter and width of fluting, and they have elaborate, bell-shaped capitals adorned with acanthus leaves. (*see also* ACANTHUS, DORIC, IONIC, ORDER)

COUNCIL Five-hundred strong legislative body that arranged the business of the Assembly. (*see also* ASSEMBLY)

CUIRASS Body armour, usually made of bronze, worn by Greek soldiers to protect their back and chest.

DEMOCRACY A system of government in which the people being governed have a voice, usually through elected representatives.

DORIC One of three principal styles (or orders) in classical architecture. Doric columns are solid with wide fluting and a plain, round capital. (*see also* CORINTHIAN, IONIC, ORDER)

ELECTRUM Alloy of gold and silver that was used to make early Greek coins. Later coins were made of pure silver or, sometimes, gold.

EPINETRON Semi-cylindrical instrument used by Greek women to prepare wool for spinning. Often highly decorated, epinetrons fit over one knee.

In fresco painting, pigments are absorbed into wet plaster to fix their colours.

Fourteenth-century fresco prepared in a similar way to those of ancient Greece

FRESCO Wall painting applied to plaster when it is wet. Frescoes were popular in many warm countries until the Middle Ages. (*see also* MURAL)

FRIEZE A deep band of decoration running along the upper part of a wall.

GALLEY Ancient Greek or Roman warship powered by one or more rows of oars.

GRAMMATISTES Teacher of core subjects such as reading, writing and mathematics. (*see also* KITHARISTES, PAIDOTRIBES)

GREAVES Bronze leg guards worn by Greek soldiers for protection in battle.

GRIFFIN Mythical creature with the head and wings of an eagle and the body of a lion.

Griffin

GYMNASIUM Large room or building used for physical exercise and training.

GYNAECEUM Women's quarters in a Greek home, where looms for weaving and children's toys and furniture would be found.

HETAIRAI Group of witty, beautiful women whose main function was to play music, dance and entertain men at dinner parties.

HIMATION Outer cloak worn by ancient Greeks. This garment was traditionally pulled under the right arm and draped over the left shoulder.

HIPPOCAMP Mythical seahorse with two front feet and the tail of a fish or dolphin.

HOPLITE Fully armed Greek foot soldier, from HOPLON, meaning shield.

IONIC One of three principal styles (or orders) in classical architecture. Ionic columns are slender with narrow fluting and a scrolled capital. (*see also* DORIC, CORINTHIAN, ORDER, VOLUTE)

KITHARISTES Teacher of music. A kithara is an instrument much like a lyre, only larger. (*see also* GRAMMATISTES, PAIDOTRIBES)

KOUROS Marble statue of a naked boy, usually intended as a temple decoration.

KYLIX Shallow, footed drinking cup with two handles.

LABYRINTH Intricate and confusing network of passages formed by walls or hedges.

LYRE Stringed Greek instrument with a hollow body that was originally made from a tortoise shell.

MURAL Wall painting on dry plaster. (*see also* FRESCO)

ORACLE Sacred place where ancient Greeks could ask their gods, through a priestess, to give them advice or to foretell the future. The most famous oracle was that of Apollo at Delphi.

ORCHESTRA Flat circular area where the actors and chorus performed in a Greek theatre.

ORDER One of several styles of classical architecture defined by shape and proportion. The three best-known orders are Doric, Ionic and Corinthian (see page 27). (*see also* CORINTHIAN, DORIC, IONIC)

OSTRAKON Fragment of stone or pottery inscribed with writing or drawing.

PAIDOGOGOS Domestic slave with particular responsibility for accompanying Greek boys to school.

Early lyre with tortoise-shell body

PAIDOTRIBES Teacher of physical exercise such as athletics or wrestling. (*see also* KITHARISTES, GRAMMATISTES)

PALAISTRA Purpose-designed building, smaller than a gymnasium, with dressing rooms and a sand-covered courtyard where Greek boys were taught athletics and wrestling.

PEDIMENT Triangular gable end on a building; decorative architectural motif, also triangular, positioned above a door.

PEPLOS An early, simpler, version of the standard Greek chiton. (*see also* CHITON)

PYXIS Small container or casket in which Greek women kept their cosmetics and combs.

Helmet protects cheeks, nose and forehead

Cuirass

Greaves

Hoplite

SLAVE Man, woman or child who is owned by another person in the same way as an item of property, usually to do work of some kind.

STOA Long, colonnaded structure with a wall on one side, where people traditionally met to talk and conduct business.

STRATEGOI One of ten elected military leaders responsible for making decisions about the defence of ancient Athens or concerning its involvement in a war.

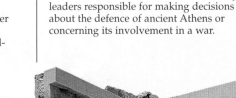

This structure was built around 200 B.C.

Ruined stoa on the island of Lindos

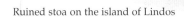

SYMPOSIA All-male drinking parties. Small, private symposia were held in private homes; when numbers increased, public buildings would be used. (*see also* ANDRON)

THOLOS Round, domed building in which the members of the government Council met. (*see also* COUNCIL)

TRIREME Fast warship powered by up to 170 oarsmen positioned over three levels on either side of the hull.

TYRANT Absolute ruler of a Greek city-state who had usually seized power by force.

VOLUTE Spiral-like scroll used on Ionic capitals and sometimes on pottery vessels. (*see also* CAPITAL, COLUMN, IONIC)

Index

Acknowledgements

Dorling Kindersley would like to thank: The Department of Greek and Roman Antiquities, the British Museum for providing ancient artefacts for photography. Patsy Vanags of the British Museum Education Service for her assistance with the text. Bill Gordon for his superb model of a Greek farmhouse on pp. 28-29. Alan Meek for the armour and weapons on pp. 54-55.
Helena Spiteri, Andrew Chiakli and Toby Williams for modelling the clothes and armour. Anita Burger for hairdressing and make-up. Gin Van Noorden and Helena Spiteri for editorial assistance. Earl Neish and Manisha Patel for design assistance.
Jane Parker for the index.

Picture credits a=above b=bottom c=centre l=left m=middle r=right t=top
Allsport: Gray Mortimore 45cl;
Vandystadt 45c.
AKG London: 66cra; Erich Lessing 64tl,
ARF/TAP: 67br; 68c; 68crb; 69bc
American School of Classical Studies,
Athens: 32tlb.
Ancient Art & Architecture Collection: 12tr, 44tl, 56cl, 63cr.
Ashmolean Museum, Oxford: 9tl
Bildarchiv Preussicher Kulturbestitz (Antikenmuseum Berlin) 33tr.
Bridgeman Art Library: 13tl De Morgan: National Archaeological Museum 3cr.
British Museum: 65tl, 65br, 67tr, 68clb, 69cla
York: National Archaeological Museum 35cr
Foundation; 18br Palace of Westminster; 20tl
House of Masks, Delos; 30tl Private Collection;
42b Private Collection; 46c

Staatliche Antikensammlungen, Munchen; 47b
Vatican Museums: 50cr
Museum Nationale, Athens; 56cb.
National Gallery, London; 58br
Fine Art Society; 60tl, 61tl.
Trustees of the British Museum: 16tr, 16bl, 16br, 17c, 17bc, 17br, 18tr, 19c, 19b, 20bl, 40tl, 47tr, 47br, 48bc, 48br Dr John Coates: 55cb.
Photo DAI Athen: 12c (neg. Mykonos 70).
Ekdotike Athenon: 52bl.
CAP: 67-68
ET Archive: 62cr.
Mary Evans Picture Library: 18tl, 26cl, 31cl, 35cr, 38tr, 39tl, 44b, 46tr, 46br, 47c, 47bc, 54c, 56tl, 56c, 56bl, 58tl, 58c, 58cr, 59, 63cb, 64br, 64bt, 69tc.
Sonia Halliday: 8tl, 11tc, 11tr, 12bl, 20tr, 25tl, 25tr, 25c, 33c, 44cr.
Robert Harding Picture Library: /G. White 16c; 38c, 49br, 52bc, 53cl, 59bl.
Michael Holford: 6tr, 7tr, 9bl, 16tl, 20br, 21c.
Hulton Picture Co: 45b.. Image Bank: 51c, 52tl, 53br, 59bc.
Kobal Collection: 63c..
Mansell Collection: 11tl, 12tl, 12tc, 62tl.

The National Gallery, London: 9cr.
SPADEM; 12br, 21tr, 22tr, 23bl, 63b.
Anne Pearson: 24br.
Photostage /c Donald Cooper: 39tc.
Royal Ontario Museum: 17tl.
Scala: 8b Heraklion Museum; 11bc, 20cl.
Museo Nationale, Athens; 24bl
Delphi Museum: 26b; 35tl
The Vatican Museums: 36tl, 38b, 41b; 44cl
MNA; 58cl Museo del Terme.
Zefa: Konrad Helbig 17tc; K. Scholz 19tr; Damm 25cl; Konrad Helbig 26tl; Starfoto 50tl; 62c.

Jacket credits
All images British Museum
Illustrations by John Woodcock and John Hutchinson.
Maps by Sallie Alane Reason

All other images © Dorling Kindersley.
For further information see:
www.dkimages.com